FRANK HERALD WATSON
Diary of World War I
March 1918 – July 1919

Transcribed and Annotated by
CAROL KAPLAN

Park Place Publications
Pacific Grove, California

All rights reserved.
Printed in the United States of America.
No part of this book may be reproduced in any manner
whatsoever without written permission from the author
except in the case of brief quotations embodied
in critical articles and reviews.

Copyright © 2020 Carol Kaplan

ISBN 978-1-953120-17-5
First Edition December 2020
Printed in the U.S.A.

Park Place Publications
Pacific Grove, California
parkplacepublications.com

PREFACE

When I took a typing class in the 9th grade, my grandfather asked me if I wanted to practice by transcribing his diary from World War I. I said, "Yes." By the time I was halfway through, I became busy with other things and never finished it.

After moving to Monterey, I asked Mom and Dad what happened to the diary. They did not even remember its existence. I guessed that it must be lost. Then years later, while cleaning out the garage, I found a box with things I'd saved from high school. In the box was the section I typed and the rest of the hand-written diary. The part I had done was in a faded black binder with yellowed sheets of paper. The original diary was in loose pages, 5 ½ by 8 inches, in blue ink, still well-preserved.

I have re-transcribed it for the family, so they can learn a little more about my cherished grandfather, Frank Herald Watson.

As you remember from my father's book about his family, Grandpa Watson had to drop out of school after the 8th grade. He was smart, but not educated. His diary had a lot of run-on sentences, lack of punctuation, and spelling errors, most of which I corrected. Otherwise it is in his words.

In some places, it appears that he went back later and wrote about what happened on a particular day.

Grandpa Watson was 39 when he enlisted in the army. I have always wondered why he decided to do so. According to my father, the English were running out of men to fight the war and were rounding up Englishmen in the United States for the English army. To avoid this, my grandfather volunteered for the Americans.

I researched the *San Francisco Chronicle* and the *San Jose Mercury News* for the first three months of 1918 and could find no stories about that. Perhaps it was a rumor.

I also questioned why he would leave Grandma at this time since she had lost two children during the previous year. My dad had no memory of his older sister, Gertrude, or his younger brother, Philip. Gertrude was born in Medford, but the state of Oregon had no record of her birth. Santa Clara County had no record of her death. From the diary, it appears that she died April 23, 1917, less than a year before Grandpa left. She was about five or six years old, according to Dad's memoir.

Records from the County of Santa Clara show that Philip was born in San Jose on January 17, 1917 and died on August 11, 1917. The death certificate states that he died of a "inanition" with complications relating to a "tubercular condition of the glands." I was curious about the cause of death. Inanition was a term that was used to explain the death of many babies in the early 1900s. It is a condition in which a baby dies because the mother is unable to adequately nurse her child. I am guessing that Grandma in her grief over the death of Gertrude may not have been able to provide sufficient milk. The term, inanition, was not used after 1920.

While working on this project, I found a number of letters Grandpa Watson had written to Grandma while he was away in the army. They reveal a romantic side of my grandfather that I never saw. I have included a few of them in this book.

- - -

A final word: The diary is not politically correct, but reflects the white male attitudes of the times. It is difficult for me to square some of his racially prejudiced words in the diary with the man I loved, but the world was different then. When I knew him, I never heard him utter any prejudicial language. I am grateful that his diary and letters survived.

— Carol Kaplan 2020

INTRODUCTION

When I think of Grandpa Watson, I remember his warm blue eyes, ready laughter, love of baseball, and willingness to be present for his three grandchildren.

I picture 68 Pierce Avenue, San Jose, California where my father grew up and where Dad, Mom, Bill and I lived from the time I was five until I was eight. Jude was born while we lived in that house. During that time, my grandparents spent the winters in Palm Springs and the summers in Oregon, where Grandmother's relatives lived. In between, they parked their trailer in the back yard of 68 Pierce Avenue.

I see Grandpa and Grandma sitting in the backyard under the giant fig tree with Bill and me on the grass, Grandpa regaling us with stories. We were curious about England where he was born, a place that seemed as far away as the moon to us. Although he had no love of England, Bill and I were fascinated by his stories of his birthplace.

We were in stitches when he took out his false teeth, something we never tired of seeing. He also sang a funny song about a monkey that we requested often.

He and Grandma were excellent card players, but nonetheless spent hours with Bill and me playing the simple game of canasta. They also taught us to play poker which we did for pennies.

Grandpa was a good cook, though he never used a recipe. On Saturday mornings, he would make pancakes in their trailer. Bill and I raced out there early to enjoy them, eaten with butter and thick maple syrup. None since have seemed as tasty.

At that time, many people had collections they prized. Grandpa collected stamps from the British colonies. He meticulously maintained them in thick binders. At one time Grandpa sold part of his collection and bought a new Chevrolet with the proceeds. He helped Bill and me start our own collections, showing us how to carefully handle the stamps with tweezers and mount them in books on special paper. He taught us how to recognize a stamp with good value. Those stamp collections kept Bill and me busy for hours. Wondering about the states and countries where they originated, I learned geography early.

Grandpa Watson had a zest for life and a positive attitude. His curiosity and openness to adventure are revealed in his diary. Though he went through hard times--journeying to the United States, soldiering during WWI, struggling with only part-time work during the Depression, and caring for Grandma as she became ill in her later years--I never heard him complain.

He loved traveling through the western states with Grandma in their trailer to see national parks, sending us postcards featuring the multi-hued Grand Canyon, the rising peaks of Teton National Park, the rushing Colorado River, among others.

When I was sixteen, he taught me to drive in his blue and white Chevy, endlessly patient as the car stuttered up and down Husted Avenue. When I started ballet lessons at ten, dreaming of becoming a ballerina and joining the New York City Ballet Company, Grandpa promised to help finance the trip.

Even when I visited him during his last years, that he spent in the Veteran's Hospital in Palo Alto, he was upbeat and had stories to tell about the other residents.

– – –

I hope the following diary and letters will give you a glimpse of this man during a year and a half of his life and a dramatic time in our world. You will read in his own words how Frank Herald Watson, my grandfather, experienced the American Expeditionary Forces, 5th Corps, 604th Engineers, Company B, where he served as a cook and became a Sergeant.

from the hand-written diary of
Frank Herald Watson

Diary Entries from March to December 1918

March 29, 1918

After work went down and enlisted at the Victory building where the recruiting office then was. Sergeant examined me, and I passed O.K. Was told to be ready Monday morn, April 1st to be examined by medical officer.

April 1

Went down to be examined and found I had to go to San Francisco to be examined, so got two hours off to say good-bye to Maud[1] and get some papers fixed up there at the Telephone office.[2] Left San Jose at 11:40 and arrived at San Francisco in time to see a big Liberty Bond Parade. Saw Margaret Joslyn in an auto with some Red Cross nurses. Then I went to the recruiting office, 660 Market St., and was given a ticket for dinner at the Winchester Hotel.

---

1 What he called my grandmother.
2 He worked for American Telephone and Telegraph, A T & T.

I was told to be back by 3 PM to be examined by the doctor. Passed exam O.K. and was taken in street car to government wharf and boarded Tug named "General McDowell" and was taken to Angel Island. There were 79 of us in the bunch. Arrived there at 5 PM and were lined up just in time for Reveille (our first) — then supper. We were then told to take a bath before being examined again. Some boys objected as they had already had one bath that day, but it did not do any good.

April 2

After breakfast, we had another examination. This one was more thorough and some of the boys had different colored chalk marks all over their bodies — looked like tattooed Indians. I had a few myself. Seems like all we did the first day or two was be examined. All but 12 of the 79 passed this final examination. A young boy next ahead of me came up to the doctor. The doctor looked at him a minute and asked how long he had been out of jail. I don't know how he knew — guess those doctors are pretty keen judges of character. It turned out the kid had only been out a week or so. He had been committed for knocking out his school teacher with a stool. They did not pass him. Some of the boys were held over until they got the alcohol out of their systems. Some of the boys went through quite a grilling, but all the Doctor asked me was who I worked for and for how long. I told him and that's all there was to that.

We all had a big questionnaire to answer. It took the best part of an hour and I could not think of anything there they forgot to ask about in your past life. We were sworn in at noon. Then in the PM we all had our finger and hand prints taken. After that we were given:

1 uniform	4 suits underwear
3 pairs of sox	3 shirts
1 campaign hat	1 pair gloves
1 overcoat	3 blankets
mess kit	brush
soap	comb
tooth brush and tooth paste	

In the evening we all moved over to "Pneumonia Point," called this because it is so cold and foggy. The wind from Golden Gate cuts right through the camp. The look-out is very pretty and you can see the lights of nearly all the cities around the Bay.

April 3

Up at 6 AM—not light yet. Had to stand in line for half an hour in bitterly cold wind and then marched to the main part of the Island to breakfast. After we ate breakfast, which was very good, we drilled for 2 hours, then had our first inoculation for Typhoid and Smallpox. One big fellow, 6 feet, who looked like a farmer, fainted. They just left him there until he got up by himself—guess they are used to that. After dinner, we had a lecture on insurance. I signed up for $10,000. $7.50 a month out of my pay. I also took $15.00 for Maud—the government making it up to $40.00.

The food is excellent. We have a large dining room holding 2500 men. Long rows of tables hold 12 men. They just dump the dishes on the table and you help yourself to all you can eat.

April 4

I went on Kitchen Police duty today for 48 hours. 70 men go on at a time. I was put to waiting on two tables and had to clean the dishes and polish spoons, etc. Also helped mop floor, but it was concrete and easy to keep clean. Mess Sergeant was named Hall and was very hard-boiled. I found from later experience that is the only way you can get by with the Mess Sergeant's job.

April 6

Was put on meat cutting and helped clean and fix 900 chickens for Sunday dinner. Asked for a 36 hour leave and got it, but as I was on K.P., I could not leave until 4:30 instead of noon. Got home by 7 PM though and found all well. They were all tickled pink to see me. Dorothy Avery was staying the night, as Mother and Katie had gone to Richmond.

April 7

I saw Mr. Brown for a few minutes, also went to visit Hartman's and just before leaving for camp went to see Father Culligan, but he was not home. Mrs. Avery and Maud saw me off at the Depot—was relieved Mrs. Avery was there to take care of Maud. Caught the midnight boat by the skin of my teeth and got back to Camp by 1 AM.

April 14

Tom Burk's sister and his girl came to visit him and I had lunch with them on the beach. While eating, camp police brought down garbage can to empty. Of course, we thought it a huge joke as they use them for latrines, and the girls had to ask what was in them. Next day, April 15, Tom Burk and a bunch left for Camp Humphrey, Virginia.

April 18

Orders came through for a bunch of us to leave for Vancouver Barracks, Washington. Had two shots for Typhoid before leaving, packed up and left Angel Island at 7 PM and went on the street car to the ferry. With our barrack bags on our backs, 22 of us crossed over to Oakland and caught the 11:30 PM for Portland. We had a tourist car to ourselves with 12 sailors who were going to Bremerton.

April 19

Stopped off at Shasta Springs for a drink of water—passed thru Medford at 5 PM but saw no one I knew. At Grant's Pass I saw Owen Reddy and got quite a lot of news about people I knew.

April 20

Arrived at Portland 7 AM. Had two hours to wait so we got breakfast in the city and walked around awhile; then caught a train at 9:30 for Vancouver—had to walk a mile from the depot to the barracks, where we were put in Casual Camp #40. The food and accommodations were very bad here. We were all entered as casuals.

April 21, *Sun. Eve letter*

Dearest Maudie

I don't know if this will reach you when I wanted it to. I think maybe I ought to have written this yesterday. Want this to reach you on the 23rd. I know you do not forget what day that is, and dearie, you may be sure I do not either.[3] *Will be thinking of you all day and also of our little darling who is in a far better world than this.*

I do not say very much, but am thinking of her most all the time I am alone. You know the English hate to show their feelings more than any other people. It is one of their greatest characteristics, and I am very, very English when it comes to that.

You must not grieve too much dearest, but think how much better off she is. Had I been at Fort McDowell I would have tried to get a pass and come home and be with you, but no doubt Mrs. A. or some of them will be with you. I think it is Katie's day off, is it not?

I hope Bernard is getting along all right, and he will keep your mind occupied no doubt. This camp is not a bit like Angel Is. I feel like the 15th Cavalry when they left Fremont and went to Arizona.

We have no drills here. Fellows have been here three and four months and don't know a single drill. They are very slipshod here, so entirely different to Fort McDowell. There are 3,000 men going from here to France today, the 318 Engineers. They are forming a new Engineers Reg., and I think we will be assigned to it.

---

3 Reference to date of death of Gertrude, Dad's older sister who died as a child.

If we are, we will be here quite a while, but one does not know a single thing about anything. We may go tomorrow and we may be here six months. Of course, as soon as you are assigned to a regular reg., you drill.

We are in the recruit quarters and have all kinds of cleaning to do.

Well, dearie, I will write you short letters often. You would rather have two short ones a week than one long one, would you not? Have you rec. a check for $114.19? If you have not, you soon will as I rec. a letter at the Fort asking me where I wanted it sent. Remember dearest, I am thinking of you all the time.

With fondest love and heaps of kisses to you both, I remain,

Your loving husband

Gertrude and Barney Watson, 1917

April 23

Was put to work for the Ordinance Sergeant and was made acting Corporal by him—had charge of four men. We cleaned rifles, boxed them up and made them ready for shipping to France.

The 318 Engineers left for France. We had a great time seeing them off. We were to meet up with them again at the front as it turned out.

April 28

Elliot, Chenswich, Epps, and Chunes left for Camp Humphrey, VA—would like to have gone with them, as we had all chummed together. Had one more shot for Typhoid and it made me pretty sick for a while. I had Corporal Patterson, in charge of sending names up for transfer, put me up for the next bunch to go East, but before anyone else went, they organized our Regiment.

April 29

604 Engineers were organized and 30 men including myself were enlisted in same under Capt. Doherty and were moved over to permanent barracks #36. Fine place, hot baths, good dining room, reading room, and sleeping quarters. Unfortunately, when I made out my questionnaire, I said I had done some cooking, so I was put in to cook with another man (Pierce).

May 2

Cook Huniziker took my place cooking at my own request and I went into ranks and started drilling. Capt. Doherty could sure put us through the paces. He also gave us a good talk saying we were in on the ground floor and there was no reason why we should not be all sergeants if we put our hearts into our job.

May 7

First pay day in 604. I received $6.30. We had our first inspection by the Commander Col. Schultz. The man next to me was named Cummins and was from Texas; he had a long heavy mustache and also dirty shoes. Col. Schultz stopped in front on him and said,

"Have you any shoe polish?"

"Yes sir," said Cummins,

"Then use it."

Then he looked up and saw the mustache and said,

"Have you a razor?"

"Yes, Sir," said Cummins

"Then use it," said the Col.

That was too much for me so I snickered.

The Colonel whirled to me and barked:

"What's your name?"

"Watson, Sir," said I.

"Well wipe that smile off of your face," and believe me I did. What made it so funny was Cummins was always fussing with his mustache and was so proud of it.

May 14

Was in the Y, but when an invitation came for a few boys to go to a private house for a social party, I put my name in. In the evening, we went—were entertained by a bunch of girls. We were only allowed 5 minutes then we had to move our chair and change girls. It was not much fun, just talking—had some eats and left about 10:30.

May 21

Woke up in the night and heard a commotion. Prosser, a San Jose boy, who has the next bunk to mine was sitting up in bed and a soldier had a gun on him and telling him to lay down and keep quiet. We had been losing quite a lot of things lately and this man was doing the robbing.

He had gone through about 10 uniforms and was going through Prosser's when he woke up. Prosser sat up and said, "What are you doing?"

The man said, "Lay down, this is just a mid-night inspection."

Prosser said, "H--- of a way to inspect, going through a man's clothes."

Then it was the man pulled a gun and I woke up. The barracks were in an uproar and Riley who slept next the door, got in the way, but the guy threatened to shoot him so he let him go and we all piled out after the robber.

A sentry was supposed to be on guard outside our barracks, but he was nowhere in sight and the robber got away; however, in spite of his hat being pulled way down on his head, several of us got a good look at him.

May 22

While eating breakfast, Riley and several others identified the man. His name was Boyd and belonged to the 318th Eng., but had been left behind for some reason. He got over $100.00 from the boys, but it was all recovered. We heard afterwards that he got a sentence of 20 years in Fort Leavenworth Prison.

May 28

All hustle and hurry today as we saw on the bulletin board that we were to leave for Washington, D.C. at 6 that evening. We marched to the depot where the band from Spruce Division gave us a good send-off. A good number of citizens were also on hand. Our company now consists of 40 officers and 80 men. We had 3 tourist cars and 2 baggage cars. We set up stores in each baggage car — one for officers and one for men. The officers had 4 cars including diner. We left by way of North Pacific.

May 29

Stopped at Spokane for a couple of hours; through Clover, Idaho at 11 AM. The scenery in Idaho is wild looking, with lots of small lakes all along the way. Arrived at Butte, Montana about dark. I was on guard at this time—had to stand guard in baggage car two hours for every six for 24 hours. A lot of copper mines around here and the hills seem all afire with the furnaces. It was a wonderful sight, the hills looked like a huge fire of molten ore, and adding to the lights from the city was a sight not to be forgotten soon. Took on a new engine crew at Butte.

The engineer sure turned her loose going down the mountain. We must have hit 50 an hour around curves and the baggage and kitchen utensils rolled all over the car. It was the wildest ride I have ever had. I could not keep my feet and was thrown from one side of the car to the other. One of the boys was thrown out of his berth and cut his cheek badly—even the conductor was worried and pulled the cord to slow the train down, but it did no good. I imagine the men were all over worked on account of so many troop trains going constantly and probably the engineer had been indulging to keep himself going.

May 30

Stopped at Bismarck, North Dakota, and the Red Cross gave us cigarettes and chocolates. Crossed the line into Minnesota and you could see the difference in the look of the farms—so clean and fine barns and comfortable houses. They looked very prosperous.

May 31

Arrived at St. Paul, Minn. At 9 AM. We backed into the yard and got off for a couple of hours drill to limber up. A school nearby called recess, so all the children could come and watch us. Crossed the Mississippi River over a very fine arched bridge and on into the state of Iowa. Stopped for a few minutes at Des Moines, and got off and had some drinks at a nearby soda fountain. This is the neatest and nicest state we have been through yet—splendid farms and swell kept and each little town seemed to have a race track just outside it. They must go in a lot for local horse racing.

Arrived at Chicago just before noon and we "monkeyed" around the stockyards for three hours. We were not allowed to go very far from the train.

June 1

Made a switch during the night onto Pennsylvania lines and arrived at Fort Worth, Indiana at 6 AM and on into Ohio about noon—tremendous lot of factories and smoke and people do not seem as friendly as they were in Chicago.

Hit a terrific thunder storm at Canton and a regular cloud burst. Some of the boys from California who had never seen or heard a real thunder storm were pretty well scared. Arrived at Pittsburg, Pa. at 9 AM--would like to have gone through here in daylight and seen part of the steel works.

We stayed at Pittsburg two hours and were given apples, chocolate, cigarettes, etc. by the Red Cross. Two big train loads of drafted men left here while we were waiting and created much excitement and cheering. The heat here was insufferable—not like our hot weather; it was a sticky damp heat. The R.R. authorities decided our baggage cars were too wide to go through their tunnels so we had to unload everything and transfer to their cars—some hot and dusty job tearing down our stoves, etc.

June 2

Arrived at Harrisburg at 5 AM and at Baltimore at 9 AM—went on right through to Washington, arriving at noon. I volunteered as one of a detail of 6 to unload baggage and put on trucks for transportation to camp. The truck driver was very accommodating and took us up Pennsylvania Ave., by the White House. Washington is a very beautiful city, so clean and the streets very wide—statues on every street corner. I was very much impressed by it all.

June 9

A lady came to camp and offered to show anyone around Washington who would like to go. A Sergeant Miller and myself volunteered to go and we had a very interesting, instructive trip. She took us through a Franciscan Monastery and also through the museum. We had some dinner and then climbed to the top of the Washington Monument, 750 feet high and we had a race up. It took us 27 minutes up and 8 ½ minutes down. We sure got a good work out—we beat the elevator up by 100 feet. The view from the top is magnificent, beautiful lawns and flowers and the stately buildings and the Potomac river gracefully flowing by.

June 10

Was made a private 1st class, raising my pay up to $33 a month. I was put on guard duty and was picked as orderly at H.Q. for Col. Schultz.

June 21

Our complement of men was filled up and we got 1,000 men from the Middle West who had been in training at St. Paul as aviation mechanics, but were transferred to us. They were pretty sore about it as they wanted to go in Aviation. Company B.C. and H.Q. were formed and I was put in as cook in Co. B under Capt. Barton—pay raised again to $38 a month; at this rate I will soon be a millionaire.

Sergeant Shearer, our Mess sergeant, used to come in and drink up all my vanilla extract. One day he hit the bottle heavy and then went out and got into a fight with a nigger and got the finest pair of black eyes you could wish for.

Corporal Patterson, who had been with us from our formation, ran off and we never heard from him again.

June 25

Took a trip to the Capitol. Went to the Senate and saw Vice Pres. Marshall, and also heard William Jennings Bryant speak. Then went to see Washington and Philadelphia play ball.

    Billion, one of the cooks, went with me. We got to the Ball Park at 2 and found all gates closed and no one around. At first, we thought we had made a mistake, but after inquiring we found they do not start until 4, in order to give government officials a chance to see the games.

June 28

Saw a ball game between Washington and Boston. Babe Ruth made a home run.

June 30

We got free tickets to this game and Clark Griffith gave away 500 bats. They were scattered all over the outfield and we were all lined up and sent our way at the gun. There were over 2,000 of us and anyone got a bat who could. I ran clear across the field and got about the last bat, in spite of a guy hanging on my coat tail. I could not beat him off and had to pull him across the field with me. The stands were packed and a bunch of us soldiers sat on the grass around the dugout. I got to talk to Walter Johnson and Joe Judge, Mays and Babe Ruth. Johnson pitched for Washington and Mays for Boston. In the ninth the score was tied and in the 10th the Babe came up and made the longest home run ever made in Washington, bringing in two men and breaking up the game, with a win for Boston. I sent my bat to Bernard. I got it autographed by Johnson, and Al Schach and some others.[4]

July 1

Moved to Glen Burnie, a Navy training camp half way between Baltimore and Annapolis. It is a Navy rifle range and has about 200 sailors stationed there. The camp was filthy. We moved in when the 603 left, and they sure left a mess. Lieutenant Col. Taylor is death on dirt and we all had to do double duty to get the camp clean — especially the kitchen crew.

July 4

Went to Baltimore. Don't care much for the city — too many slums, streets narrow and buildings dark and dirty. Went to a big amusement park and had a good time — everyone helps you if you are in uniform.

---

4 Bill Watson remembers seeing the bat, but its whereabouts now are a mystery.

August 4

Out on target practice with sailors for instructors — shot at 200-yard range and made 89 out of a possible 100 — slow firing 5 shots lying down, 5 kneeling, 5 squatting and 5 sitting down. At rapid fire same positions made 75 out of 100 points. We only had 30 seconds to fire 5 shots, made marksmanship easily as 150 was all that was necessary to qualify and I made 164.

August 10

I tried the sharp shooter course and made 20 points at 200 yards, 20 at 300 yards, 21 at 400 yards, and 19 at 500 yards. I had to change position after each shot. Then I started back after 500 yards, ran 100 yards back, reloaded and had to shoot within 1 ½ minutes, repeated same at 300 and 200 — only made 71 points here so did not make sharp shooter this time, but came within 4 points of it. Being in the kitchen did not help me any as I did not get the proper exercise.

    A funny thing happened during inspection of tents. The camp Sgt. was taking the Colonel around inspecting tents, and as we get up early to cook, we do not police-up our tents, so when the Colonel came to our tent it was in a mess — no bunks made and clothes all over the floor. He turned to the Sergeant and said,

    "Whose tent is this?"

    "The cooks," said the Sergeant.

    Then the Colonel bawled the Sergeant out good for taking him in there and we got off scot free.

August 22, 1918 letter

Darling Sweetheart:

Fancy you working in a grocery store. Be careful dear and don't stay on your feet too much. On no account do any heavy lifting. You have some experience in the different kinds of work. This work will be good experience for you, as you will know of some different kinds of foods to buy. When I get home shall expect some new dishes to eat. You are not a bit more glad to rec. letters than I am, especially from you. I remember that grocery very well, but don't remember the people. Have been in the store once or twice.

Today we finish turning in all our old issue clothes. Last night at retreat the Lieutenant told us what we could take along. We can take one woolen sweater and anything that does not materially increase the size and weight of our pack. I think we will probably move out of here by Sunday or Monday. By the time you receive this I will be at Camp Merritt, but continue to write here and the mail will be forwarded to us.

We are not allowed to take any American money, but have to change it to Travelers' checks. We are not allowed to send any sealed letter after reaching port of embarkation. If you write a letter and leave it unsealed so it can be read by the censor, it will go, but all sealed letters will be held until our safe arrival at the end of our trip.

Sent the mosquito netting home. Thought it would be nice on Bernard's cot, if it is outside. I had it given me so do not have to turn in. As they are worth about $4.50 a piece, it is worth sending home.

There is a man coming tonight to change our money into French money, so we are evidently going straight to France and will not go to England. I am sorry as I should have liked to train there awhile.

If you should have to write to the War Office about anything regarding me, this is the way you address my name: Cook Frank H. Watson (522110), Co. B, 604 Engineers, A.E.F., and that is the way you will address your letters after I get across. A.E.F. stands for American Expeditionary Force.

Enclosed list of things we have to take along. Thought you would like to see it. Sent pictures of whole Co. home yesterday and hope it arrived safely. The officer with two bars is Capt. Barton.

Will write again in a day or two. We may be here for a week yet. It is hard to tell when we will be out.

With fondest love darling and kiss B. for me,

Ever loving <u>Hun</u>

August 23

We the 604, were training for Pontoon Bridge Bldg. and on this day, we had a contest between the Companies. We had to build a bridge over Chesapeake Bay or rather a neck of it—250 feet across. We had to carry the boats on to the water and place our planks in position and then have all our wagons and horses and equipment across.

B Company took 23 minutes 13 seconds. A Company, 26 minutes and C Company, 27 minutes. We then took apart the bridge—B Company in 14 minutes 17 seconds, C Company in 16 minutes 25 seconds and A Company in 17 minutes. We won that. In building water-tight canvas boats, B Company 2 minutes 50 seconds, A Company 4 minutes, and C Company 3 minutes 30 seconds. A Company won the boat drill,

B Company was second and C Company disqualified. Boat race—C Company 1st, B Company 2nd, and A Company 3rd.

B Company came out miles ahead in points and we were all given 3 days leave of absence. I hear Capt. Doherty of A Company gave his men an awful dressing down for their poor showing. Glad I was transferred to B Company.

Rolling Chairs on the Boardwalk, Atlantic City, New Jersey

August 25

Had our 3 days lay-off and started for Atlantic City with Private Carlsen. We had special rates—1 cent a mile. Some of the boys went to N.Y. and some as far as Boston. Left on the 9:30 for Atlantic City. Arrived in Philadelphia at noon and had to stop over for 2 hours—saw a little of Philadelphia and then on—

Arrived at Atlantic City at 3 PM. All the people on the train were swell telling us all the best places to see, etc. Atlantic City was packed. As it was a week-end, we were fortunate to get beds at the Y for 25 cents—only men in uniform were allowed in. Lots of people with money in their pockets had to sleep in the park on benches. Had a simply glorious time—very few soldiers there and all the girls fell all over themselves showing us a good time. There is a million-dollar fun house out on one of the piers and you can have a barrel of fun there for the entrance price. Went swimming in the ocean and on Sunday walked along the 3-mile boardwalk—Wowie—what swell dressers there were parading after church.

All the big stores and famous hotels face the ocean and you walk between them and the ocean on the boardwalk; so, there is plenty to see and enjoy. Left Sunday at 10:30 PM. Had to change at Philadelphia again. The train we changed to came from N.Y. and about the longest passenger train I had ever seen and filled up to the brim—had to stand up all the way to Baltimore. Arrived back in camp at 6 AM Monday, after one of the best trips I had ever taken.

August 29

All the men who were not naturalized had to go into Baltimore and become citizens. A batch from each separate country went up together and were sworn in—35 of us were from Great Britain. This was the last time we could leave camp as we were under orders to leave for France.

August 30

Everyone packing up getting ready to leave. We could only take certain things, so extra shoes and personal things we thought we would like, we packed in a box and marked "Kitchen Utensils"—just the kitchen help did this; however, it did us no good for we never saw that box or any of our camp equipment again.

The last evening, we had a shirt-tail parade, and Jackie, one of the cooks, led it, without a stitch of clothing on. Don't know how we got by as there were any number of visitors there and the girls were hiding their heads on the shoulders of their soldier boyfriends. When we got to the sailors' quarters, they turned the fire hose on us and we got a soaking. The sailors turned us in and tried to make trouble for us, but Colonel Schultz was a good scout and paid no attention to them. Over half the regiment took part in it, so I don't know what they could have done anyway.

August 31

Made 600 sandwiches for B Company on the trip—had an early supper and fell in with full packs at 7 PM. Stood in line until 8:30 when we started loading and left Glen Burnie for France. We left on a Friday and had 13 coaches on the train (if anyone is superstitious). Went through Delaware which is just one mass of factories.

September 1

Arrive in New Jersey at 9:30 AM loaded on to a ferry boat and fooled around until 12 noon when we landed on a wharf and the Red Cross gave us one small bun and a cup of coffee. Then we boarded the Cunard Line "Carmania" which was to take us across. By the time we located our berths, etc. it was too late for dinner so we had to wait until supper. We were all on the second sitting for supper and it was 6:30 before we ate. Our berths were down in the bowels of the ship and we were packed in like sardines—over 3,000 soldiers on the one ship.

A battalion of colored soldiers were on the ship and had all 2nd class cabins and nice dining room and all the best of everything. The 900 niggers had the best half of the ship and 2,100 whites had the rest. I guess they would have had trouble with the niggers if they had been below; they would have been scared to death. We were anchored alongside the "Aquatania" at that time, the largest ship in the world.

September 2

At 8 AM we pulled out of dock and anchored out by the Statue of Liberty until 3 PM then started our trip. Again, some thought for the superstitious mind — there were 13 ships in the convoy and we took 13 days to cross. We had 4 destroyers, 1 battle cruiser, and 6 airplanes as convoy for us. The airplanes and battleship left us but the destroyers stayed until we were met by British destroyers. We had to wear our life belts all the time and sleep with our clothes and boots on.

The food on board was atrocious. Some of the fish we ate was almost rotten — we all kicked but it did no good. We could not eat the food and most of the boys were hungry all the time, so we renamed the ship the "Starvemania." Some of the boys who had money never went to the tables to eat, but lived on the canteen.

September 3

Reveille at 6 AM — felt rotten on account of the close quarters and bad ventilation. Saw a submarine and the destroyers fired 6 shots at it, but it disappeared. The destroyers whipped over to where it submerged and dropped depth bombs, and from then on, we took a zig zag course changing every few minutes.

September 12

After an uneventful voyage, we are nearing land—several funny incidents occurred during the voyage. Someone asked what made the white caps on top of the water and one man from the middle west said it was the salt. I got a kick out of that.

Guy Berg, one of my cooks, was the only one I saw that was really sick. The ocean was choppy, but we were on a big boat. Some of the other boats were having a time of it and were rolling considerably. On nearing England, we took the northerly course. It was very cold and windy, and lots of mist—almost like a rain. Tonight, we were ordered to stay on deck all night as we were in a very dangerous zone—submarines and mines. A convoy of 24 English destroyers met us and our destroyers left for the U.S. no doubt to bring another convoy over.

September 13

Sighted the north coast of Ireland and a little later the Isle of Man. It was very foggy and we could not see much, but the land looked mighty good to me after our cramped quarters. Came to anchor off Liverpool at 11 PM.

September 14

We stayed at anchor all day, and we watched ferry boats go by crowded with people and going over to New Brighten to the beaches. The busses with their double decks looked interesting and we all crowded to the sides of the ship to see all the sights. All the rest of the ships unloaded, but we just anchored out there for some unknown reason. We landed at 9 PM in a drizzling rain and walked to camp Knotty Ash 5 miles out of Liverpool. We were ordered not to make any noise on the march, but we were all so tickled to get off the boat that we hollered ourselves to death on the way out. Landed in Camp at 11 PM, had hot coffee. The camp was up to your knees in mud. We were huddled in tents with just a board floor and no bunks. We were crowded 20 to a tent and the only way one could get room to lay down was to lay with his feet towards the center of the tent. Only 3 thin blankets and laying on wet boards. A lot of men got sick in this camp from cold and damp.

> THE SHIP ON WHICH I SAILED HAS ARRIVED SAFELY OVERSEAS.
>
> Name *Frank H Watson (Cook)*
>
> Organization *Co B. 604th Eng*
>
> American Expeditionary Forces.

September 15

We were to have moved out of here today, but orders got mixed and another regiment went in our place. It turned to be lucky for us as I heard they got badly cut up at the front. Grub was very poor here. In fact, all the English camp gave us poor food and not half enough of it.

September 24

Received a 2-day furlough to go and see the folks. Caught the 9:30 PM from Grand Central. Burgers got a leave also and accompanied me. We got to London, Marylebone Station at 3 AM and had to walk to King's Cross about 3 miles, in black-out and pouring rain. Got there about 4 AM. — no train for Muswell Hill until 7:30 so had coffee and doughnuts at a Y hut and slept on a bench until train time. There were lots of sad scenes at each stop from Liverpool — English soldiers saying goodbye to their loved ones as they started back for the front again after having a furlough. I had to change trains at Finsburg Park and it recalled the many times I changed there on my way to and from school, even to the commuters who were waiting in crowds for their trains.

We had come a long way since then and it did not seem possible that there was a war on. One of my school mates, George Wright, who used to commute with us was one of the first to lose his life in the war.

I was travelling from London to the suburbs so there was no crowd going my way. At Crouch End a young lady, munition worker, got in my car and while talking with her, found she was going right by where I wanted to go, so had no difficulty locating my sister's house.

Maybe Gertie was not surprised to see me. They did not even know I was in England. I had not seen any of my family for 15 years. Gertie looked just the same only very much heavier. We both went over to see Nora and family. Nora was really fat, much more so than Gertie. She has a fine family. Eileen the eldest girl is very pretty — Eric and Frank were away. Eric was playing the leading part in a show called "The Boy" and was playing in Liverpool. When we arrived there, had I known, I could have seen him. It was only one week's engagement there so I lost the opportunity. Nora has grown so like Mother, except in weight, that I could hardly keep my eyes off her. Sent a telegram to Father, and at 5 PM he arrived at Gertie's — found him looking very much older, but still very spry. Father was very much overcome when he saw me. When I left England the first time, he was in the hospital undergoing an operation and I really had not seen him for over 20 years. Latham came in later and looked just like the pictures of him. He did not impress me as amounting to much—he stutters quite a lot.

In the evening, we went over to Nora's and I saw Frank—the same old Frank—full of the devil. His hair has turned white but outside of that the same. They had company, some British Officers and other Swells and I felt out of place in my private uniform and hob nail boots. Nora's second girl, Kathleen, is a dear and very talented. She goes all over the country playing for the soldiers. She is a great mimic and had us in screams nearly all the evening. She is only 15 years old.

Molly and Vera, the youngest ones, are both very sweet and took quite a shine to me. They would not go to sleep until I had come up and kissed them good night. Could not get to see Katie, George, or Emily. They were too far away.

Our family did pretty well. Father has a commission as Capt. and is in the pay master's office at the War Office. George is in Aviation so that accounts for all our men in the immediate family. After saying "Goodbye," Gertie came on the bus as far as Highbury. I told the conductor to let me off at Marylebone Station, but he took me on to Paddington. As everything was pitch dark, I did not know the difference. When I did find out I had only 10 minutes to catch the train, so I grabbed a tube train and just made it by a hair's breath. Got back to Knotty Ash at Reveille.[5]

---

5 There were six children in Grandpa's family: Katie and Nora were the older two sisters. George and my grandfather in the middle. Gertie and Emily were the youngest. My grandfather was especially fond of his sister, Gertie. After the war, he sponsored her and her son Peter to come to the United States. They lived in San Jose and frequented the house on Pierce Avenue.

FRANK HERALD WATSON—1918-1919

September 30

Went to Liverpool to see a League Football match. Liverpool vs. Aston Villa—did not get much kick out of it and left before the end. No seats—everyone stands up. The ground is sloping so everyone can see, but it is awfully hard to stand on it. Went to the Midland Hotel and got a good hot bath. The maids thought I was staying there and one maid told the other to get some towels for the officer. They drew the water and fixed things up fine and I really enjoyed that bath about as well as any I ever had. Had not had a decent bath since we left Baltimore. Must tell a funny incident at Knotty Ash:

Lieutenant Schroder was always snooping around the kitchen and we wanted to get rid of him, so we planned a trick. We got to talking of weights and one man said that he bet he could tell the Lt.'s weight if the Lt. would get on his back. The Lieutenant never dreaming anything was going on (he being an old Army Sgt. who was promoted) got on the man's back with his arms around the man's neck. Billion, a cook, is a big husky man, weighs about 200 and all solid. He got a paddle that they use to fish pies and bread out of the oven with and brought it with a crash as hard as he could on the Lieutenant's behind. The Lieutenant gave one yell and beat it. We never saw him around the kitchen again. He didn't say anything about it as he had no business around there anyway.

During our stay at Knotty Ash we had a Corporal, Corbett by name, break out of camp. Our camp had a 10-foot steel fence all around and people outside would peer in through the rails. It made us feel like monkeys in a zoo. Well Corbett scaled the fence. One of the officers saw him and called him to halt, but he kept going. Then the officer fired his revolver over

Corbett's head, but it did not stop him. However, Corbett was captured in Liverpool and brought back. He was confined to the guard house for the rest of the stay at Knotty Ash and his Corporal's stripes taken away.

October 1

Stayed up all night making sandwiches for the trip to Southampton. Boarded train at 6 AM. We had breakfast at 4 AM, passed through Birmingham and Oxford. Saw the universities from the train, through Reading and Winchester to Southampton. Boarded boat at 5 PM and arrived at La Havre in the night sometime. We were packed in the steamer like sardines. Absolutely no room to move and a pretty rough voyage, too.

October 2

Unloaded at 7 AM, had to walk 3 ½ miles with full packs uphill most of the way to the camp. We went from 4 AM when we left Liverpool until 12 noon the following day on 2 sandwiches and 1 orange. Our packs weigh 60 lbs. A lot of the men fell out and could not make the camp at La Havre on account of weakness. Very poor arrangements as they had coffee and food ready for us on the boat, but we were not allowed to have it.

La Havre was another English camp and we had cold meat and bread for dinner and fish every night and tea at supper time. We did not get enough food to keep a rabbit alive. Slept on boards, 20 in a tent as usual, but we were getting used to it. As long as we had money, we could always buy some grub at the canteen.

We lost quite a few men at Knotty Ash and La Havre with sickness. There were a bunch of Australians at this camp, and they were fine fellows. We taught them to shoot Crap and they had lots of fun with us — more like Americans than anyone we had come across yet.

October 5

Left Starvation Camp (La Havre) at 8 PM, walked to La Havre and boarded train for the front. We were herded into box cars half as big as ours, 40 men to a car. We could not all lay down at one time and cracks were in the bottom where the wind whistled up, some cracks were 1" wide. We all suffered severely from cold and discomfort on that trip. We could not sleep at all.

October 6

Passed through St. Cyr and Versailles and outskirts of Paris.

October 7

Passed Chatillon and Chaumont. Had one more sleepless night. We lived on hard-tack, cold corn, beef hash in cans, tomatoes and cold water all the time we were on the train.

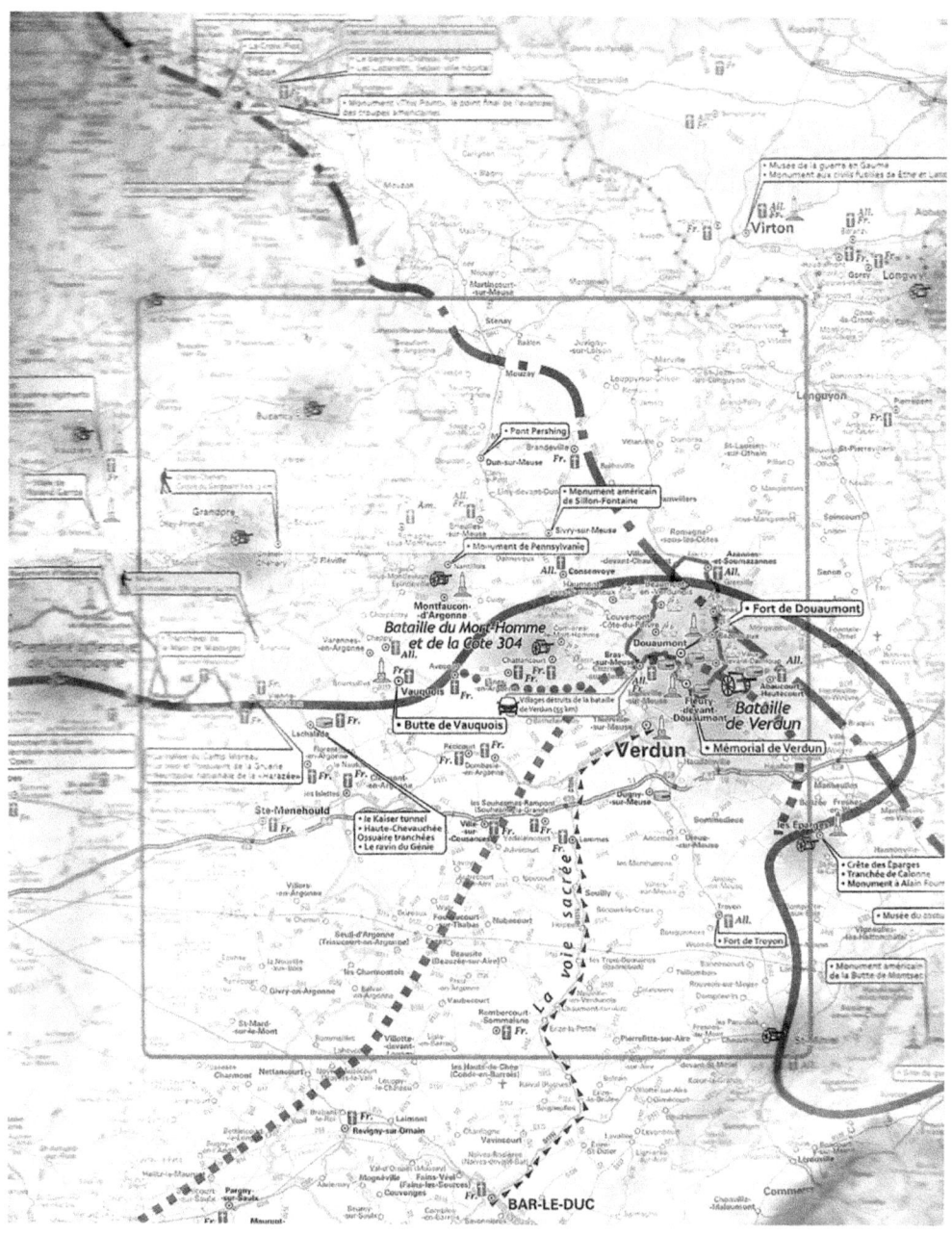

October 8

Arrived at Port-de-Artillier about 2 AM. Had some hot coffee and corn willie and started on a 12-mile hike to Cornot. H, Q, and C Company went 2 miles further to Lavigne. We cooks had a fairly good place to sleep in, an old house near the kitchens. A Company cooks stayed in the same place.

I got good and sick at the stomach here. Too much cold corn beef hash and cold grub. However, I got well again as soon as I got all that trash out of my stomach by vomiting. Stayed in bed a couple of days.

October 10

Felt lots better and started to cook again. Grub fairly good here. Could get lots of eggs from the French people. Had one of the boys who could speak French go with me and we cleaned up all the eggs in the country—80 centimes a dozen.

October 14

Davis started cooking for our officers' mess. Sorry to lose him as he was a good cook and hustler.

October 18

Took first bath since leaving Liverpool and it sure felt good. Mess Sgt. McClellan of B Company got drunk in the evening and lay down by the stove. The officer of the day came by, saw him and turned him in. He was demoted. Davis wanted his job and I heard that Davis has been getting pie, coffee and sandwiches for Captain Barton every evening while we were in Baltimore. He was getting in the good graces of the Capt. Mac had been getting drunk there and making himself obnoxious. Davis knew it would be only a matter of time before he lost his job and Davis wanted it badly. The captain wanted to give it to him, but I had longer service. Also, I heard that quite a few of the Sergeants spoke a good word for me, especially Sergeant Diddier, who had been a Mess Sergeant in the regular army, so the Captain had me in his H.Q. office and told me I was to be Mess Sergeant at $46 a month.

He told me he knew Mac was getting drunk in the U.S. and he overlooked it, but we were in a foreign country and at war and those things could not be over-looked. He was going to put Mac in the ranks, but I asked him if I could have him as one of my cooks, so he let me.

October 19

We received our first mail since leaving U.S. September 1, and was there rejoicing. Received 5 letters from Maud and a lot from the folks in England.

October 20

Received my warrant as a Sergeant also gas masks and rifles. We also had to go through the gas house to test our masks and see if they leaked. The gas smelled like garlic. It was the crying gas. We all got an awful kick out of the French toilets in the streets. They are all open facing the sidewalks and have a 12-inch board across so passers-by can see from your shins down and waist up. It is very embarrassing until you get used to it.

October 28

Left Cornot at 8 AM. Put up our stoves and cooked dinner at Port De Artillier and left there at 8 PM—32 in each box car. Sergeant Shears got back from the hospital where he had been sick since we were at La Havre. He told us he was taken for dead one morning and they put him in a coffin and draped the stars and stripes over him ready to take him away. Fortunately, they did not nail him down and pretty soon he came to and nearly had a fit when he saw where he was.

October 29

Arrived at Clermont at 6 PM. This is the end of the line and we are up where the fighting is. We are only a short way from Verdun. Put up our tents. Everything was pitch dark and no light allowed. We got to bed when I heard Capt. Barton roaring, "Sergeant Watson." I got up and went to his tent. He said, "Breakfast at 7 AM Sgt." That was a mess. The stoves were in the baggage cars, no wood, no water, a strange land and pitch dark.

Well I figured we would have a lot of that thing from now on, so I routed out my cooks and K P's and we set to. Of course, our stoves were in a far corner of the car and we didn't have a light as we would have been blown to pieces had we shown one. I do not know to this day how we got all our stuff out and wood and water gathered, however by midnight we had it all set up and ready. Big guns on 3 sides of us were roaring and shaking the earth and lighting up the sky in the distance. Kept us awake all night.

October 30

Up at 5:30 AM and started to build a fire for 7 o'clock breakfast. Had it just good and going, when out pops Major Young and rushes over yelling, "Put out that fire, do you want us blown to pieces?" So out goes the fire. He started bawling me out, but after I explained it was Capt.'s orders he quieted down and told me never to make a fire until day light.

We were assigned to the 5th Army Corps under General Liggett. Saw our first air battle. A German airplane came over head and our airplanes chased it, but were not fast enough. Anti-aircraft guns sent 16 shrapnel shells after it. You could see them burst and the smoke hang in the air, but none of them came anywhere near the enemy plane. The smoke from the shrapnel was sulphur colored and would stay in the air 10 minutes or more.

October 31

Moved our camp into the woods nearby on account of German planes locating our position. Soon after we had moved some enemy planes came over and dropped bombs right where we had been located. Seven U.S. planes went in pursuit, but again the Germans were too fast for them. Had our first visit from cooties and rats in camp.

November 1

Another battle in the air right over our head, causing lot of excitement — no casualties though. Moved again. Once more nearer the front. We are getting to be expert at setting up our kitchen equipment; one move, we struck camp at 4:30 PM and by 5:30 we had the men eating a hot stew and stewed prunes and coffee. The Captain complimented us on our speed. He came over and said, "Very snappy, Sgt. — fine work." I told him I had a fine bunch of cooks and KP who knew their jobs and were not afraid to do them.

    Capt. Van Ness was made Mess officer in place of Lieutenant Staby. I was glad as I like Capt. Van Ness. He has been with us right from Vancouver. He was the officer who gave us our last swearing in there. He said at the time that now we were really U.S. soldiers.

November 3

Moved again up into the Argonne forest, near Varennes. We lost our way and landed in Cheppy, but we finally got where we were supposed to and had to make camp in the dark.

November 4

Moved again to Hill #304 called by the French "Cigarette Butte." Could not put up our tents but slept under a tarpaulin. It poured all night and we got soaking wet.

November 6

Moved into dug outs back of Dead Man's Hill, named this on account of the awful slaughter of both Germans and French in their effort to capture the hill — 40,000 Germans and French were killed around here. The French had been trying to capture this hill for 4 years unsuccessfully. It took our boys just one drive to clean them out. This hill was considered an impregnable stronghold. All the trees around here are cut off by bullets right down to the stumps and the whole country is littered with French graves.

November 7

Took a trip through the inside of Dead Man's Hill. This hill is catacombed with tunnels all fixed up with concrete floors, electric lights, fine sleeping quarters, and massive timbers to keep from caving in. There were big turbine engines, and generators and thousands of gallons of bottled water for drinking, tons of ammunition and every imaginable comfort, even to pool and billiard tables.

The 91st Division helped take the hill and lost a lot of men here. At the base of the hill, there had been a town named "Vauquois," but there was not a stick left of it. The French tunneled under the mountain and set mines using hundreds of tons of dynamite and blew the town and half the hill into space—leaving a hole 300 feet deep in the middle of the hill. There must be hundreds of thousands of dollars-worth of wire around here all in a mass of entanglement.

November 10

Two train loads of French refugees passed through here this morning. It was a bitter cold frosty morning and the poor people were on flat cars, and not much clothing. Some were so cold they fell off the cars from exhaustion; young 14-year-old girls with babies and some expecting them. It was pitiful and made my blood boil. They stopped near our camp and I made a big boiler full of coffee and gave it to them. We have a lot of grief in the kitchen as we are repairing the narrow-gauge R.R. that sends provisions up to the front.

We have details coming in all day and night to get fed. The trains go through at night and we have to see everything is in shape. I send out 200 lunches each day. We have a cook named Harold Johnson and he is a railroad man and carried a Union card. Al Johnson got chummy with them and when they got to our camp they slowed down and Johnson used to get a couple of quarters of beef and some sugar, oatmeal, rice, or anything he could lay hands on and throw it near our camp. We would pick it up, so we really fed well while here.

After a while they began to miss this stuff and our Capt. asked me if we ever raided the trains. I said a couple of times we had found things on the ground that had fallen off. This is just a narrow-gauge R.R. and very crooked and insecure. Lots of times a whole train would turn over on it.

Took a walk with Sergeant Snorf and we went to Cheppy, 3 miles away. This town is badly cut up and deserted. We saw hundreds of German prisoners filing by on their way to concentration camps. From Cheppy we went on to Varennes. This is where Louie and Marie Antoinette were captured fleeing from the French Revolution. This town is also badly cut up even worse than Cheppy. Had a cup of cocoa at the Red Cross and it sure tasted good, about the best I had ever tasted. Walked on around by H. and Q. who are stationed at Neuville, and on home. We walked in all, 14 miles.

Our menu at this time was: for breakfast: Oatmeal mush, bacon, coffee, bread and syrup and hot cakes, and the men kicked like H—l because we did not get enough hot cakes. For lunch we made them up and took out. For supper: roast beef or steaks, bread, potatoes, corn, cake and coffee. Of course, we could not have done this without the extra provisions Johnson wrestled up for us. We are fed better than any outfit on the front and still the men kicked.

November 11

Armistice Day — but we did not know of it until the next day.[6]

Dearest Sweetheart,[7]

We have been moving around so much lately, that I really have forgotten when I wrote to you last. Each time we moved we got nearer to the front and also it got harder and harder to get material to write with. The supplies do not seem to get up to the front where they are needed most. They leave that to the Salvation Army and Red Cross. When it comes to entertaining at home or in England, the Y is right there, but when it comes to giving stuff away the Red Cross and Salvation Army are the ones to look to. You can buy from the Y, but a soldier would starve to death if they waited for the Y to feed them gratis.

Well we moved four times in one week and believe me I got sick of it. We are in very comfortable quarters in French dugouts on what was one of the fiercest conflicted grounds in the whole line. We have electric light and running water and stoves in the dugouts and also millions of enormous rats. Just across the next hill is where the Germans were camped for three years. I have been all through the tunnels they made, and they fixed it up to stay: concrete floors and timbered up better than any mine I ever saw. Big turbine motors for power, electric lights. The officers' quarters were fixed up like a palace: pool room, a wine cellar with thousands of bottles of wine all sealed. This was down a shaft 500 ft. deep. We did not touch it. In fact, it is dangerous to touch anything as you never know it might be connected up with a battery somewhere and would blow up the whole mountain. There are thousands of cases of all kinds of ammunition and explosives.

---

6 Though the war ended, many troops, including the Engineer Corps, stayed to repair roads and bridges.
7 Written on thin paper like tissue paper, no date.

And you ought to see the hill, all torn to pieces with shells and mines and explosives. It's a wonderful sight, trees cut right in half. Every few yards you will find a French graveyard with all the way from 10 to 500 graves. They sure had lots of fighting here. The towns around here are simply battered to pieces. Some of them have not even a wall left standing.

Yesterday I got a pass and took a 14-mile walk with another fellow and we saw some sights. One town had a big church with 3 walls left standing. It looks so awful. Lots of the inside was intact and we could see some statues.

At noon we got hot cocoa from the Red Cross free, and it sure tasted fine. The first I have had since leaving home. The water here is abominable. It all has to be boiled and chlorinate of lime put in it to make it pure. Well we tried to get a paper and could not. We are way off the main thoroughfares. We never get papers or anything. Of course, we hear much of the news. I can imagine how glad and thankful you were when the news came about the armistice.

On the road we met about 1,000 German prisoners, and they were a rotten looking lot. They made me think of a show at home in London called Madam Tussauds, where they have wax models of all celebrities. They have a chamber of horrors where all the noted criminals are. These fellows reminded me of that. I can quite imagine them performing all the atrocities said of them. They sure look it.

Excuse the paper. I had a hard time getting even this. We have no idea how long they will keep us in this country or where we will go. I guess they are very unsettled yet.

The other day two train loads of French refugees went through here. They were riding on flat cars. Had been on them 24 hrs. We are getting hoary frosts every night. They sure suffered a lot. Not nearly enough clothing. All the girls over 14 had babies in their arms or were expecting them. It made me wish the war would go soon so we could exterminate the German nation. I got them hot coffee and something to eat. It was the best we could do for them.

We have not had any mail since leaving Carnot. That is a month ago. Hope to receive some soon though.

Hope you are all well and that Bernard is still increasing in health. Give my love to him and tell him to be a good boy.

With fondest love and kisses,

Harold

November 18

Was foraging around and came across 2 U.S. soldiers lying side by side. Looked like they had been killed by the same shell. Must have been dead a month and the rats had eaten nearly all the flesh off them. Their dog tags were intact, and showed their names as Chas. Nelson and Silva Hagestande, both of Company G, 364 Inf., 91st Division. The draft # was in the 3 million, and they came from Camp Lewis. A bible in one of their knapsacks showed they came from St. Louis, Minn.

I turned their tags over to the Capt. Must have been some heavy fighting around here as there were plenty of crosses where our men had fallen. There were lots of rifles and equipment around here, left on the ground.

November 19

I went down with a detail and buried those two men and put 2 crosses up. The rats ran around in a circle about 30 feet away while we were burying them. The rats around here are the biggest I have ever seen—and more of them. One ran over my face one night while I was sleeping, but I did not sleep any more that night.

November 21

We got 3 days furlough. That is all the Sergeants got in details of 6. Lieutenant Stirling took Sgt. Diddler, Hoesington, Ead, McNair and myself and we left at 8:30 for sight-seeing. Walked to Aubreville, caught a ride in a truck to Verdun, had dinner at a casual camp and walked around the city. It is well fortified and has a wall and moat around it, like the cities of old times. The walls were 20 feet high, what was left of them. The streets are very narrow, and there was not a window left in the whole city from the awful bombardment it had received. Went through what was left of the Cathedral and convent. Left Verdun at 3 PM and caught a ride on a truck to Arracourt, 10 miles. Had supper with the 154th Infantry, then on their way back to the coast. They had been hiking for 7 days and had 15 more days to hike before reaching their destination.

After supper we decided to walk on some more, and by doing so I missed seeing the 411 signal corps. We passed all the boys from San Jose in the dark. They were camped along the road we were walking. I would like to have seen Champ Graham and Pinkie Tustin. We walked 6 miles to a big town called Etain. Everything here was blown to pieces, but we found a place to sleep in—the vestry of a church. About the only thing we could find with a roof on it. We took turns keeping a fire going as it was bitterly cold.

November 22

Rose at 5 AM. Had some hard tack, jam and water for breakfast and started out again. Took a wrong turn and started N towards Belgium for 2 miles before we found out our mistake. Cut across country to Buzzy, 5 miles on and waited there for dinner. We ate with the 29th Engineers. Rode in an ammunition truck to Conflans, 7 miles and then walked on to Doncourt, 4 miles. This was the German H.Q. during the 4-year attack on Verdun. We stayed at a farm house all night and we found a lot of swell souvenirs here. It had evidently been occupied by some German high officers.

The Huns had only left the place a few days before we arrived, and we got rifles, helmets, epaulettes, buttons, etc. We also found a sack of spuds and we had baked spuds for supper. They were very welcome, along with our hard tack. Our jam was all gone.

We meant to get up at 5 AM, but the beds were too soft and we all slept until 7. Had hard tack and water for breakfast and walked to Montegry. Passed into Alsace Lorraine at a town called "Gravelotte." From Conflans on you would not know there had been a war. Farms all well kept up and all the towns we went through were celebrating. From Gravelotte on we saw lots of graves of Germans who had fallen in the Franco-Prussian War, and lots of monuments to officers who had fallen in that same war.

From Doncourt to Montegry is 12 miles, and we went through some very beautiful country, especially as we neared Metz. At Montegry we caught a street car into Metz. We were all glad to get a ride as we were all of us about all in. We had been throwing away our souvenirs as the going got tough. I don't think I ever enjoyed a ride better. We created quite a sensation in the car as we were the first Americans in Metz except for the M.P.'s. The only other way we could have gotten in was by street car, as all the roads outside Metz are being patrolled by American M.P.'s to keep soldiers out.

We arrived at Metz at 11:30 AM and we were supposed to be back at camp again that evening as our furlough was up. We figured on getting a train out of Metz but found all transportation was tied up. We were surrounded with people all the time we were there. We could have had all kinds of souvenirs if we could have stayed long enough, but the M.P.'s caught up with us. We were only allowed to stay and eat dinner and then beat it out again. We ate at a place called Lune Café in the City Square. We had a small portion of meat, potatoes and a bottle of wine—no bread for bread was rationed and you had to have a ticket to get it. The meal cost us 49 francs, and we could have eaten six times as much. After dinner we took a look at the Cathedral. The Kaiser's statue in there had hand cuffs on it. Also, all the German monuments in Metz had been knocked over. The streets were very narrow, but what we saw of it, it seemed a nice clean city. Sgt. Diddier and I left our rifles in the café after packing them 18 miles. It's lucky we did, as we had a long walk back. Anyway, we got so many better souvenirs that we discarded the rifles. We bought some bread, one franc a loaf, and 4 lbs. sausage, 16 francs, and started back for camp at 3 P.M. A French band was playing in the square as we left. Would like to have listened to it. Walked to Gravelotte 10 miles and caught a truck, which fortunately for us had lost its way coming from Germany. We rode as far as Conflans with it. We ate the sausage and bread while riding. Just outside Conflans we found a galvanized ammunition shack and stayed there all night. It was so cold none of us could sleep, and of course we could not have a fire in there. We got up at 3 AM, had some bread and cold water for breakfast and started for Buzzy thinking of the nice breakfast and hot coffee we would get from the 29th Eng. When we got to Buzzy, we found it deserted. Everyone had left, so we bottled our disappointment, pulled in our belts another notch and started to walk again. We were all pretty weary by now. We walked to Elaine, where by good luck we caught a truck which was going right through to Varennes. We got out a Neurilly and walked a mile and a half to our camp. Arrived at 2 PM after one swell trip which with all the hardship I would not have missed for anything. We were the only ones to get into Metz although others tried it. I had a German helmet and Lt. Buckingham offered me 100 francs for it, but I refused, and have been sorry lots of times since that I did.

November 26

Went on a foraging raid to see if I could locate anything extra for Thanksgiving. Went to HQ and then on to Varennes. Got 150 lbs. cocoa, 200 lbs. sugar, 2,000 pkts cigarettes and 100 magazines. Also bummed 2 days rations from HQ at Varennes. Had Cottle and Swanson come over with a truck and load up.

November 27

Got an extra ¼ of beef for Thanksgiving. I tried to get it back with a cart. The road was so bad, could not, so had to get a truck. It rained heavily for 2 days.

November 28

Thanksgiving Day

Had braised beef, gravy, mashed potatoes, corn, cocoa and prunes for Thanksgiving dinner. About 2 PM heard a tremendous explosion. Found that Usilla, our bugler, had been monkeying with a hand grenade. He had picked it up and it went off blowing him to pieces, also severely wounding Evans. Although Evans had one eye out and badly wounded in body, when we got there, he was trying to help Usilla.

November 29

Buried Usilla at Varennes in the US cemetery. Evans lost one eye and was badly wounded, but he finally recovered.

We have a detail who go out and get wood and water after supper as it gets dark quickly. I let them in ahead of the men's line in front of the sergeants. Sgt. Wasil made a row about it and took it up with the Capt. I got an awful bawling out from Capt. Barton for letting anyone in ahead of the non-commissioned officers.

November 30

Had orders at 3 PM to get ready to move at 7:30 AM next day. Made sandwiches all night. At 11 PM the bugler blew fire call. The orderly room and a lot of dugouts caught fire. Lots of excitement as shells began to explode and all the hillside looked to be on fire.

December 1

We had so much equipment we could not haul it all, so left a lot of stuff behind. We moved by wagons hauled by horses and the going was so tough that they could not haul much. Went by way of Aubreville to a town called Florent, 6 miles west of Neuville. Reached there at 3:30, unloaded the stoves and set up in an abandoned shack with half of the roof blown off. Had supper ready by 5:30. Florent is a fair-sized town, filthy dirty and ankle deep in mud. The water is abominable, like all the water in France is. I had pretty good quarters here. Shared a room with Sgt. Hamilton and buglers Erickson and Ostram. We had bunks and a good fireplace.

December 7

Had orders to take our rolling kitchens out on a hike. Had to tear down our tables to get the stoves out. Took everything but our field ranges along. We all thought we were leaving for good. We were all good and mad after hiking 10 miles to have to turn around and come back again. The water carts were ordered filled. The horses got stuck on a hill and the cart had to be abandoned for the time, so we had no water to cook with when we got back. When we got back to Florent we found the French people had raided our camp and taken everything that had been left, thinking we were gone for good. Big bunch of the boys got drunk that night on cognac and French wine.

December 8

Borrowed a horse from stable with Sgt. Hamilton. He and Sgt. Snorf and myself went to St. Meuchold. Met our band Sgt. Harry Johnson, who was on his way back from the hospital in Paris. He said GHQ sent him to Bordeaux and said to wait for us there as we were on our way home. That made us feel good as we expected to get orders any day for home. Then he said the 57th Eng. went home in our place, so we did not go after all.

St. Meuchold is the biggest city we have been billeted near since coming to France. Streets narrow and stores small. Tried to locate a place to eat, but the French only serve meals at 12 noon. It was after 1 PM then so we had to go without. The Germans got into St. Meuchold and stayed there only 12 days. Then our boys drove them out. There is a French cemetery with 18,000 French soldiers in it located here.

December 9

We receive our rations from Les Islettes, the nearest RR depot. It is about 9 miles from Florent. Our rations were pretty slim here: dried potatoes and vegetables in 5 gal. cans. They did not taste very good. The prunes we got were just a pit with skin around it and wormy at that. We were the last Reg. to leave anywhere near the front and there were not many rations sent. We got bacon instead of beef.

December 10

Went to St. Meuchold and got a suit of underwear, socks and a swell suit of pajamas from the Red Cross free. Had a good dinner at a restaurant. When we had eaten it, we called the waiter and told him to bring on another dinner just like that. And we ate it, too. Roast veal, mashed potatoes, beer, hot coffee, bread and cheese, and only 5 francs, 75 centimes. Walked home in the rain and got a real soaking.

December 11

Took an all-day hike. Cooked dinner on rolling kitchens, while on the march. We had the stew in a fireless cooker, and it did not work well. The stew was only warm and was not a great success. It was beginning to go sour owing to being kept from the air. Another hour and it would have been unfit to eat. We had stew, hard tack, prunes, and coffee. Everything went off good in spite of pouring rain. Everyone got wet through. Got back to camp at 3:30 PM. Sgt. Hamilton skipped this march and Major Young found out. He went to the stables and asked Sgt. Hamilton why he did not march. Hamilton and the Major had soldiered together on the Mexican border. Sgt. H. could not give a good excuse so the Major had him lift up every horse and mule's leg so the Major could examine their shoes. We had over 50 of them, so I guess Hamilton got a good workout.

December 16

Cottle got a day's leave of absence and came home very drunk. He stayed that way until I had to put him to heavy duty outside. I got Baker in his place as KP. Went after another field range. Took a truck and went to a salvage dump and got a range, 2 GI cans, 6 containers. Then went on to Clermont for hay. Had none there so went on to Varennes. Everyone had cleared out of there except the Colored regiments who were salvaging stuff. The Colored boys were handling grenades, etc. carelessly and we told them what had happened to our bugler and like to have scared them to death. They wanted to quit right there. Coming home we passed 200 tanks in a field all lined up for inspection. We heard the next day the President was through there inspecting them.

December 18

We had another all-day hike. Billow took a dozen potatoes with him and baked them on the way.

December 20

Had our first snow storm since coming to France.

December 23

Rations getting mighty short. Went after some more but could not get anything but hard tack and canned dried vegetables. In our last bunch of rations, we had 6 cans of fancy chocolates. As there was only enough for ½ chocolate a piece, I decided to let the cooks and KP have them. Sgt. Justice found out I had received them and went and told the Capt. He called me up and asked me about it, so I had to lie. I told him I had never received any candy. He said it's a good thing anyway as candy was no good for the men. So, I got out of that neatly. Hated to fib, but I did not want to lose my commission.

December 24

Christmas coming and no provisions. Went to St. Meuchold and tried to buy some food, but could not. Then went to Verdun with a truck and got potatoes, cigarettes, cigars, cookies, candy, and canned peas and also a 200 lb. hog. We got all of this out of our mess fund. The stuff the folks home read about turkey and big Christmas dinner may be so, but I *never got it*. If we had not had a mess fund to draw on, we would have had canned corn beef and hard tack for Christmas dinner.

December 25

Snowing all day. We had roast pork, applesauce, brown potatoes, dressing, creamed onions, peas, cake, dates, one cigar and 2 pkts. cigarettes, and some candy for each man. Stayed up all night cooking for this feed. C Company and HG just had corn beef and hard tack. Their mess Sgts. went to wrestle up anything. Everyone in B Company was satisfied. The officers all complimented us and said we did exceedingly well. Went to midnight mass and wrote a long letter to Maud. We put in a miserable Christmas. Slosh and mud all over the place. The band came over from HQ and played for the boys during dinner, and said they really did it for the benefit of the cooks of Company B. A motor cycle rider came in after dinner and presented me with a toilet bag given by the Red Cross for the mess Sgt. Several things I needed badly in there, including a new deck of cards.

December 29

A bunch of niggers from a neighboring town came in here and got drunk and started a row. Scotty Embleton, one of our MP's, shot and killed one, and scared another so badly he dirtied his pants. The guards ran him into a horse pond and made him wash himself. There was ice on the surface of the pond so he really got good and cold. What with fear and cold, one would think he had the ague.

December 30

Sergeant Justice had a room to himself near the cook house. We ran him out of it and put a range in and made it much warmer and lots more comfortable to cook in. We are gradually getting fixed up pretty good. Suppose we will move again soon.

December 31

Had a show battle. B Company against A, C, and HQ. B company won, but I almost got mine. Was baking a cake and had to pass over an open cellar with a plank across it. Just alongside there was a brick chimney standing all alone. I suppose the jarring of the guns weakened it. Just as I passed over the plank, down it all came. The cellar was about 6 ft. deep and it filled up with bricks. I was so close, some of the bricks hit me. 3 seconds earlier and I would have been under the whole pile. Also, some 8X8 rafters 30 ft. long came down and just missed me.

New Year's Eve. Stayed up all night and saw the new year in. Capt. went inside car to Chalons and got another hog. Our supplies are getting less and less all the time. Have used up all the extras we got off the trains at Barricade. QM moved from Les Iclettes and we have to go all the way to Clermont for rations. Had another big row with niggers at St. Meuchold. One MP and 3 niggers killed. All US troops forbidden passes to St. Meuchold.

Diary Entries from January to July 1919

January 1, 1919

Had about the same kind of dinner we had at Xmas except for cookies and candy, cigars and cigarettes.

January 4

All the supplies I can get now are canned corn beef, bread, sugar, and beans, also coffee. No vegetables, butter or syrup. Heard a rumor that the boxes of stuff we sent from Glen Burnie were at Verdun. Sgt. Hamilton and Murrey went after them, but it was a false alarm.

January 5

Dodge car came in with an officer from HQ at supper time. At 7 PM the Capt. sent me a note saying we would move in the morning.

January 6

Walked to Les Iclettes and cooked dinner in the rolling kitchen. Train was to have arrived a 2 PM. At 3 PM Major Young sent word to have supper at 4 PM. Had no wood, no water to cook it with, but had hot coffee and cold corn beef by 4:15 PM. Train finally came in at 7 PM. Loaded all our kitchen stuff in a car and the cooks and myself got in with it. We had more room than the rest of the regiment. We had US box cars this time and the rest of the boys went 75 to a box car.

January 7

Arrived at Chaumont 9 AM. Gave out corn beef and hard tack for breakfast. Arrived at our destination, Rolampont 11 AM. Stood around waiting for trucks until 3 PM. When we loaded up and set out for Villiers-Sur Suize, 9 km out. Our truck got stuck in the mud and we did not get there until after dark. The men all walked out there with full packs and no dinner. Most of them were all in when they arrived. I took 4 cooks with me on the truck to help set up, but McLean, our former mess Sgt. beat it when we got there. Got drunk just when I needed him most. Had supper by 8 PM. I gave McLean up as a bad job and turned him over to 1st Sgt. who put him in the Co. No wood here again and had to cut up lumber from a shack to get supper and breakfast. We have to pack all our water by hand up a hill about 4 blocks until our horses and water can get here. We have barracks here, but no stoves. It is mighty crimpy. The Suize River runs through this village. Women go down there and wash their clothes in the river, with snow on the ground. They have a big rock roughened and scrub on it. This village is very pretty. The Germans did not get this far. It is the cleanest town we have been in yet, although there are manure piles outside each door. The bigger the pile, the more well to do they are. Part of our equipment and some stoves were overturned in a ditch half way here. Both driver and helper got drunk and ran into ditch. Found one stove 2 miles back from where the car overturned. Our rolling kitchen got the wheels smashed, so that let us out of any more all-day hikes. Company C moved on to Neujorirs to work on roads.

January 12

Horses and wagons arrived. Davis went to work in the kitchen cooking again. Taylor going to cook for the officers.

January 20

Furloughs were being given out to go to Aix-les-Bains. I wanted one to England, but was informed by the Capt. that we would be leaving for home before I could get one there, and I had better take this. So, I put my name down. My furlough was granted. Only 27 in our Company were going.

January 26

Notice read at supper to be ready at 5:30 to go to Aix-les-Bains. Started at 6:30 in open ammunition truck for Bourbonne-les-Bains, a distance of 60 miles for the train. Rode until 11:30. Nearly froze to death. Snow on the ground and thermometer at about 16 degrees. Then had a billet in a small room with no beds, eight in a room. Slept or tried to on bare floor with only one OD blanket. Just before leaving the mail came in. I got a Xmas box from Maud, cookies and cake, candy, etc. It was only one month late arriving. Also received letter and cards from the folks in England.

January 27

Train was to have left at 7:30, but we waited until 6 PM before we got aboard. That's about all we do here is wait on the French. They are terrible. I managed to bum a swell meal off of a Casual Co. stationed here. Being a mess Sgt. gave me some prestige as I was the only one that got a meal. We got left all around as we travelled in the night. I would like to have seen a little of the country. We had dilapidated old cars, all windows broken. We stayed in the depot on the train until 1:30 AM when we finally got under way.

January 28

Stopped a while at a place called Groix at 9 AM. Had some bread and jam and cold water for breakfast. Arrived at Lons-le-Saunier at noon, Bourg-en-Bresse at 3 PM, and Aix-les-Bains at 5 PM. Twenty-three of us went to the Hotel le Alboun, a real swell hotel. There were 800 of us on the train, most of them from the 29th Division. Had a real supper and a swell bed, sheets and all. First time I had slept between sheets in 9 months. Corp. Campbell and cook Berg shared my room. The casino has been taken over by the Y and all kinds of games and amusements were going on there.

January 29

Took a trip down to the town of Aix-les-Bains. Visited the Temple of Diana built in BC 58 by Julius Caesar. A lot of the wall is still in good state of preservation. Then we saw an archway built by a Roman general before the birth of Christ. Next we visited the 7 hot springs. Italian engineers in 1865 tried to find their source but could not. It is run through tunnels in a ditch to the baths. The water is 115 degrees Fahrenheit and runs at the rate of 60 miles an hour. You can hardly bare your hands in the water, it is so hot. Saw an old bath the Romans used 2,000 years ago. Then went over to the modern baths. Saw J.P. Morgan's suite of rooms there, and also the bathing rooms of the Crown heads of Europe, including the late Queen Victoria. There are 17 different kinds of baths here, and all hot sulfur (natural). In the afternoon we saw a couple of really good vaudeville shows at the Casino.

Went to Chambery. Train as usual was 2 hours late. Looked over the castle where the old Duke of Savoy used to live, and saw the old Cathedral. This is the town where Hannibal made his headquarters on his way across the Alps to capture Italy. He used elephants to cross with. Chambery is the capitol of Savoy Province and is very much bigger than Aix, but it has not the wonderful hotels.

January 30

After breakfast had a hot sulfur bath. These are all free to US soldiers. The best bath I have ever had. In the afternoon we went to the top of Mt. Renard, a trip I would not have missed for anything. Took an hour and a half. Some places it was so steep, we could hardly keep our seats in the RR train. The train is run on cogs. The snow was just right for skiing. I put on a pair of skis for the first time. Had a barrel of fun. Got nicely tangled up several times, and furnished lots of fun for the boys watching me, as most of them come from Minnesota. They were brought up on such things. One place in the mountain you could look down almost a sheer 4,000 feet over a precipice to the valley below. This mountain is only 5,070 feet, but on a clear day you can see Mt. Blanc and Hannibal's Pass. The view here is unsurpassed. Was late getting to the show at the casino, so the Y man put me in a private box belonging to the Duchess of Savoy. Hadn't been there 5 minutes when in came the Duchess and her party. Wanted to leave, but she would not hear of it. Made me feel quite at home. I sure was some bumpkin that evening. They were all in evening clothes (some stuff).

February 1

Took a trip to D'Hautecombe Abbey. Had to walk 3 miles to steamer and had 11 miles on Lake Bourget. This abbey was founded by St. Bernard in 1125 AD. Saw his tomb there. Also saw tomb of St. Antony Felix, one of the early Christian martyrs. All the Kings of Savoy are buried here from 900 AD up to Charles, the last king of Savoy in 1826. The painting on the ceiling of the abbey is the most wonderful I have ever seen. It was done by a noted Italian painter 100 years ago and looks like it was only painted yesterday. It looks so fresh. Another interesting thing is the chronology of the Kings of Savoy, all sewn on velvet by hand at the head of each tomb. Dates of birth, death, and length of reign. In the PM I hunted for souvenirs. Bought some silk for Maud and also some medals.

February 2, Sunday

Went to church AM and PM. In the afternoon I listened to a concert at the Casino by the 1st Army Corp Band, one of the best Army bands in the US.

February 3

Went to Chambery again hunting souvenirs this time, but could not find much that I wanted. Colored soldiers have a good canteen here and you can get a swell meal very reasonable. In the evening we had some good boxing bouts.

February 4

At 1:30 we went down to HQ to check in, 35th Div. Were told to entrain at 7:15 that night. 29th Div. and 5th Army Corp were told to watch the bulletin board for further orders.

February 6

At 3:30 PM we got notice we were to leave at 7:30 PM. I had to report at QM at 4:30 and take charge of rations for our bunch. Got the rations and returned to depot at 7:15. Got a detail to help me and distributed the rations in each compartment of the train. Left Aix-les-Bains at 8:45 after one of the nicest vacations I have ever had. The Lieut. in charge picked out one of the best cars for me and 5 other sergeants. 2nd class, cushioned seats. We had plenty of room to stretch out. Arrived Dijong 8 AM. In Sur Lille at 10:30. Red Cross handed out some bread and coffee there. We were side-tracked here until 3 AM the next morning. Snowed all day and was bitterly cold. At Is-sur-Telle while side-tracked, a freight came by loaded with milk. As it was going very slowly, one of the boys in the next compartment grabbed a 5 gal. can of milk, so we had lots of milk to drink with our hard tack and jam. If we had only found some way to heat it, it would have been twice as good.

After being side-tracked 17 hours (time does not mean anything to the French), we arrived without further adventure at Bourbonne-les-Bains at 3 PM. We took 12 hours to go the last 50 miles from Is Sur Lille. Waited 2 hours for trucks and then borrowed 9 from the 29th Div. They took us to Nogent, HQ for the 5th Army corps, where we found our truck had passed us on the road. Had to wait until 9:30 before our trucks came back. Arrived at our camp at 11:30 frozen stiff. The trip to and from Aix-les-Bains sure took the joy out of the rest of the vacation.

February 9

Found the acting mess Sgt. had drawn 10 days rations and used them all up in 8 days. We had nothing but bread and meat which we got every meal for two days, and of course I got all the blame for that from the Co.

February 12

Orders came through this morning to move again, this time to Montgey-le-Roi, about 60 miles away near Chaumont. The whole regiment moved in trucks. Arrived about 11:30 AM. This is the first time we have ever come in a new place early enough to get things straightened up before cooking supper. I was going to load a bunch of wood for our first meal. Capt. Barton said there was plenty of wood over there, but when we arrived, found the usual thing—no wood or no provisions to get any. I traded a lot of Bull Durham to a Frenchman living near the billets for enough wood for supper and breakfast. This is quite a nice little place, about 2,000 inhabitants. The streets are wide. It is several miles off the railway. The cooks and myself are billeted across from the kitchen, over a stable. Comfortable quarters. The teamsters did not come with us. Since they had to have a cook, I got McLean back from 1st Sgt. Miller and put him in to cook for the teamsters. President Wilson on a tour of France had his Christmas dinner in this town. Spent the evening with the people who own the house under us. They are the nicest people I have met yet in France. Diddier is the name, and Madam made waffles for us and gave us coffee. She had a daughter 12 years old, Madeline. They cannot speak much English. She gives us milk twice a day and also eggs when she has them. There are two cows, chickens and hogs under our quarters, so we have the healthy smell of the farm under us at all hours.

February 17

The boys arrived with the horses and they tell me they had a time with Mac, as he was drunk most of the time. The second batch of boys for furlough left for Nice today. Would like to have gone there as it is so nice and warm there and on the Mediterranean Sea. Cook Jackie and Sgt. Hamilton left with this bunch.

February 21

Capt. Barton came in at 9 AM on an inspection tour and as 8 days rations had just arrived and the cooks and KP's had had their teeth inspected this morning, the place was a mess. The Capt. would not take any excuses and I got a real dressing down.

February 22

Capt. Barton left for a 3-day vacation in Pons. It was market day here today in Montgey. They have a live stock market once a month. Lt. King gave me 200 francs out of the mess fund to buy extras with. Got 25# coffee, 1 can milk, 1 can jam, 1 case corn, ½ doz. pkts. of corn starch, 10# butter, and 1 case rolled oats. Came to 193 francs in all. Our mess house is situated near the forks of two roads and we get lots of stragglers and truck drivers in to meals as they can see our kitchen from both roads. We get all the extras. I guess word gets around that I feed the men well. One bunch of truck drivers after eating said it was the best meal they had had since coming to France. We had a lieutenant on special duty eating with us for a month. He would not eat at the officers' mess or hotel. Said he got better food from us. He would sit on an empty case and eat off another. Said he would rather do that than eat anywhere else off a table.

March 1

A truck went to Chaumont and I took the opportunity to go and get some extra supplies. This is Gen. Pershing's headquarters. I saw him several times at Chaumont. There are more generals and cols. than buck privates here. I saw the guard changed. It is a grand sight, and the finest band in the US Army.

March 2

Capt. Barton left us to go to Bonn University near Paris to learn mining engineering. He came down to the mess hall and shook hands and wished me all kinds of success.

March 3

Woke up at 3 AM to the tune of pigs squealing and found that Madam Diddier was crating little pigs to send away. The roosters usually wake us up about 5 AM every morning with their crowing.

March 5

We received a new field range and turned in our old rolling kitchen. We also drew out long pants and had to turn in the old regulation britches, which I think was a dirty shame as we had the britches ever since we joined up.

March 13

Today was our 6-month anniversary of landing in France and we are entitled to wear a gold stripe on our sleeves. Bought a pig. Paid 1,071 francs for it. We put on a big feed: pork and dressing, cake and cherries. We also bought gold stripes for each man out of our mess fund.

March 15

Went to Chaumont again. Miss Williams our YMCA girl came along and got a lot of supplies for the Y canteen. I could not get many supplies as there were six bags of mail besides Miss Williams stuff. We also had 3 of the boys with us. Saw the guard mount again. The band has 60 pieces in it and played while guard was being inspected. Also, there were 20 buglers and drummers. They played in between pieces. It was most impressive. Saw General Pershing twice today. Went down to the aviation field and saw the King and Queen of Belgium come in, on a visit to General Pershing. Saw Sec. of War, Baker, also. Had my picture taken with Sgt. Hamilton along side of some captured German planes.

Sergeant Frank Watson (left) and Sergeant Hamilton. U.S. airfield at Chaumont, France, 1919.

March 21

The men have been working at the Quarry nearby getting out rock for repairing French roads. Today they started 2 shifts. We have one breakfast at 4:15 AM and the second at 7 AM. Dinner 11 AM and 12:30 PM. We also have to put up lunches for both shifts. Makes a long day, but I have two shifts of KP's and I work Mac nights. He gets the first breakfast.

March 23, Sunday

A bunch of us got together and asked the Capt. for a truck so we could go to Domremy, the birth place of Joan of Arc. We got it and started a 10 AM. Had a swell trip. We got to Neufcheteau in time for dinner, which we got at the Y station there. Saw the town and at 2 PM we went to Domremy. Saw the cottage where Joan of Arc was born. Bought some souvenirs and then went to the church dedicated to her. Upstairs they have a picture gallery and saw life size pictures of the most important events of her life. The pictures were magnificent. The different expressions on her face were simply wonderful and especially the last one where she was being burned at the stake. The agony expressed on her face was almost human. Went back to Neufcheteau and loafed around there awhile, and then home. I don't know when I enjoyed a trip more. On the way home we passed the biggest base hospital in France. In all the trip was 120 miles.

April 2

Went to Chaumont with Miss Williams and Miss Darlington, also Sgt. Dolquist and Witham. We broke down ½ mile from Chaumont and had to walk in. Bought some supplies out of our mess fund: milk, jam, apples, etc. This is payday and we have the usual amount of drunks. Mac as usual got on a barrage. I had to get up out of bed and throw them out. Had a time with them, but got the MP's to help me.

April 5

Invited Miss Williams and Miss Darlington to supper. Gave them a real American dinner: T bone steak, mashed potatoes, and made a dried apricot pie especially for them. Did they enjoy it. They live and eat at the French Hotel, so it was a real treat to them. They ate out of our mess kits and got a big kick out of it. Then they got in line and washed their own mess kits in the GI cans. First hot soapy water, then hot rinse water. When they left, they said, "Please won't you ask us up again. We enjoyed it so much." Taylor came back to cook for us again today after cooking for the officers for a couple of months.

April 6

Taylor and I were invited down to a French dinner where the officers eat. Mademoiselle Keweya, two nice looking French girls, Cecile and Germaine. We had rabbit cooked French style and it was fine. The girls can both talk English well and have lived in Paris a lot. We sang all the latest songs and had games until 11 PM.

April 7

Started at 10:30 for Langres. Arrived at noon. Langres is built on top of a plateau, 450 ft. above the surrounding country. It is the oldest town of Gaul, built in 57 BC. The cathedral was built in the 12th century and St. Martin's Church in the 13th century. There is a figure of Christ on the cross which was carved in the 14th century. It is said it was modeled from a notorious thief who was crucified on purpose to get the model for this figure. This is in St. Martin's Church. There is also another, the Roman church of St. Dizier which is also very old and in a fine state of preservation.

April 17

Went to Bourbonne-les-Bains for supplies. Mess Sgt. Miller of A Co. came also. Got some canned milk, sugar, chow chow pickles, macaroni. Got all this extra out of our mess fund.

April 19

The boys on the morning shift all got drunk on the job and the French MP's came out to get one of them for some offense he committed. The boy ran them off the place. Lt. Sterling went out on the job and found half the gang had gone to Nogent, instead of working. The whole regiment is pretty sore at having to stay over here and manicure French roads instead of going home. The officers sympathize with them and close their eyes to a lot that is going on.

April 20, Easter Sunday

We had services at 9:45 on top of a hill overlooking miles and miles of beautiful country. Chaplain Kemp held services and the Regimental and

National Colors were placed each side of the altar. About 400 of the boys were there. It was very impressive with all the boys. Kneeling in the open, the regimental band played the music for mass. A Co. had a firing squad and B Co. furnished the buglers who blew taps after mass was said. It was a glorious day, nice and warm. At 11 services were held in the Y, which I also attended. We had a dandy speaker. At dinner we had a few of the boys raising H—ll as they had taken on too much cognac. It spoiled the impressiveness of the day for me.

At 1:30 there was a truck going to Langres, so I hopped on and we got there in time for services at the Cathedral. They had a procession of 30 priests in different robes. It was all very interesting. Was to have left at 8 for camp, but drivers did not show up until 9:30, the worse for liquor. We had a wild ride down the dangerous hills in the dark, but arrived home safe, mostly owing to a kind providence and luck.

May 11

A neighboring French family had communion services for their children. Davis, Stoker, and I were invited to Madam Flammarion's to a banquet in celebration in honor of her twins, Rose and Cecille. Davis and Stoker wanted to back out, but I persuaded them to come. There were about 60 at the banquet and each of us was given a nice French mademoiselle to look after us. We had lots of good eats, cakes and several kinds of wine. After a few drinks of wine, I got up and sang Tipperary and several other songs and got a nice hand. We had champagne, cognac, sherry, port, etc. so no wonder I could sing. The party broke up at midnight.

FRANK HERALD WATSON—1918-1919

May 14, Letter

Dear Son,

This is to wish you many happy returns of the day. On your next birthday, daddy will be home to help you celebrate it, I hope.

I am sending you a little souvenir of France. Keep it and when you get bigger you can say your daddy sent it to you from Montigny-le-Roi, France on your 4th birthday. When Daddy comes home, he will bring you something better.

Be a good boy and do what Mother tells you and you will please your Daddy. That's way better than any way I know of.

With lots of love and kisses, Sonny,

from your Daddy

May 15

Had a show here at the Y called Coast to Coast Six. One young lady was from Calif. And I asked her what part. She said Los Altos. We got to talking and found she is a cousin of Perking who works in the Central Office here in San Jose. She is also related to Mr. Halsey, one of the directors of the A T and T. Her name was Miss McDowell. She knew a lot of people in Palo Alto I knew. It was sure fine to be able to talk about the folks at home. The show itself was one of the nicest and cleanest we have had. We had dancing after the show.

May 16

Had a shot in the arm, 3 in 1, also physical and cook inspection preparatory to leaving for home. My arm was good and sore for a few days, and it also made me feel pretty sick.

May 18

Had orders to prepare for 1st move towards the good old USA. Trucks will be at camp at 7 AM. Had to make sandwiches for the whole Co.

May 19

Had breakfast at 6 AM. Trucks arrived at 9:30. Loaded up and said goodbye to Madam and Madeline Diddier and the rest of our friends there. They all took it pretty badly and hated to see us go. We had 60 trucks in the escort. The dust was terrific. We arrived at Rolampont, a concentration camp at 1:30. The 603rd engineers were just moving out to go to Le Mons. Ranges were already up at this camp, so we started cooking.

May 20

Had orders to move to Le Mons at 6 AM next day. 605th Engineers and 23rd Engineers left here today for Le Mons.

May 21

Up at 4 AM. Had breakfast and policed the camp, and incidentally got a good bawling out from the Capt. because he said it was not clean enough. Marched to depot and entrained at 8 AM. US box cars this time and we had the stable detail in our car. As usual they wanted all the room and we had considerable scrapping before settling down for the night.

May 22

Arrived a Le Mons 5:30 PM. Unloaded and walked ½ mile to camp in deep sand with our packs on our backs. What with souvenirs and rifle, it was all of 85 lbs. Toughest hike we had had yet, although not far. Located tents and had to hunt up some old ticks and put straw in the for beds. Had supper at 9:30 PM. A Co. cooks were in charge tonight. Corn beef hash, bread and coffee was all we had. Facilities awfully poor here. No wash rooms and very little water. Lots of soldiers to use what little there was.

May 24

We quit work at 9:30 AM and C Co. relieved us. Stood physical and cootie inspection until 9, then slept until noon. Drew summer underwear and filled up all shortage in equipment.

May 25

Final inspection by the permanent camp officers. Spread our equipment on the ground in front of us. Our Co. B was highly commended by the commander. He told our Capt. that outside of one small unit of medicos, ours was the best supply of equipment he had examined. Equipment very neat and all in the right place. Men's appearance and clothes very neat. Only one man did not come up to standard. Kreidler did not have any dog tag. We got 99% efficient. When he came to me, he told the Capt. to have me turn in my rifle to the supply Sgt. as a mess Sgt. had enough grief without having to pack a rifle, and I agreed with him heartily. Then we went over to the shower and had a special to kill any cooties which were overlooked. We went through in double quick time, 70 men in 4 minutes. Then in the PM had to start in to cook again. Had 16 cooks and 45 KP's. Co. C relieved us again at 7:30 the next morning.

May 26

Up at 5 AM. Breakfast and then a hike to a small town called Spey, 7 km. out of Le Mons. We were to wait here until boat arrives at port for us. This is a very pretty part of France. HQ Co. and Co. C shared one camp and kitchen. A and B shared another. We only had 3 field ranges to cook for 500 men and everything was most inconvenient. We had to beg, borrow, or steal wood to cook with. I had to go 4 miles out in the country to buy some wood to cook with. We are billeted over the Cure's house. Stone floor. We have bed ticks and straw to sleep on. There is an abundance of small fruit and hay in this part of the country. The people are much higher class than at Montigny, Le Roi, and Argonne. No manure piles in front of the houses here.

May 29

Just got in our day's rations when orders came through to move on to port. Used as much as we could for dinner, our last meal. Assembled at 1:30 and marched to Le Mans. Entrained 56 men to a boxcar and left at 6:30. The 605th Eng. went along with us. We are now called the 129th provisional regiment, being formed from the 604th and 605th Engineer regiments. We have a cook car on the train. We had a hot supper and breakfast for the boys.

Passed Morlaix at noon. This town is 185 ft. below the RR and a bridge goes over the top of the town. Arrived at Brest at 1 PM. Had dinner at the dock and then marched to Camp Pontenanzen, 3 miles up a hill. My pack weighed 85 lbs. when I started, but before I got there it was all of 85 tons. Am glad I got rid of my rifle when I did. Started raining and when we got to camp there were no provisions made for us. We stood in the rain over 2 hours while they were trying to find room for us. Looks like as long as this camp had been running, they would have had some kind of a system.

May 31

Lay around camp doing nothing much. All my duties are to round up 1 cook and 13 KP each shift day and night.

June 2

Move inspections. Very thorough this time. An officer inspected each article of clothing thoroughly, as we filed by. One officer for shoes, one for breeches, etc. We came through in good shape. A base hospital unit left to board a boat for home, and on the way down some of their boys shouted to MP's, "Who won the war?" They were turned around and sent back to camp. The 318th Eng. went in their place. Believe me, when our time comes, we are sure going to keep mum.

Got a pass and visited Brest. Found it quite a city, the largest we have been in since coming to France. It is just like the rest of France in one respect, everyone out to bleed the boys from the USA and get all they can out of us up to our last franc. A lot of US battleships and destroyers in the harbor here.

June 4

General Pershing, his son, General Butler, Sec. of War, Daniels, and General Wood inspected camp today, and reviewed the 808th Infantry Regiment, a colored outfit. They certainly balled things up in great shape. One Co. started marching off the field before General Pershing left. A staff officer had to go after them and bring them back. We spectators got a great kick out of it. I would hate to be in the Captain's boots, though. I bet he got his from the regimental commander, as everyone knows, no one is allowed to leave a reviewing field before the commander-in-chief.

June 5

One hundred of our Co. B were detailed to help load boats at the dock.

June 8

Had temperature test for fever. Got paid today. Maybe they thought being paid would bring on a high temperature. Also had physical and cootie inspection. The cooties are sure getting H-ll these days.

June 10

Up at 4 AM. Turned in 4 blankets and policed up tent. Started for boat at 6 AM. Arr. at dock 8 AM. Red Cross gave us sacks filled with chocolate, cigarettes, etc. for the trip. Got on a barge and started for the Battleship New Hampshire which is to take us back to God's country. Off at noon on our voyage home. Everything quiet and no trouble. The sailors on board do everything for our comfort they can. The meals are excellent.

June 11

Woke up feeling a little bilious owing to rough sea. We made 296 miles the 1st 24 hrs. A little foggy and high wind. We had lots of fun slinging our hammocks and more trying to get into them. They are slung about 5 ft. high. You get in one side and roll out the other before you know it. Once in, you can't turn very well and that does not suit me.

June 14

Passed the Azores Islands today about 4 PM.

June 15

We sighted a floating mine today. Ship stopped and lowered a boat to look at it. Then the boat fired a few volleys at it, but they did not take effect, so boat was recalled. A 3 in. machine gun was fired from the deck of the ship. 1st shot blew it up. It made plenty of noise and scared lots of the boys that were not aware of what was going on.

June 18

One of the sailors took me all over the boat. First in the firing room. There are 12 stoke holes, each having 8 furnaces. They only have 7 stoke holes going at one time, making 56 furnaces. They have a dial that rings up the number of the furnace that needs coal, so the fireman coals up whenever the bell indicates the number of the furnace. Next I looked over the shafts. Oil is pouring on those continually. Also, a nag is across the bearings and water flowing continuously on it all the time. Went through the dynamo rooms and also into the elec. room that works the big guns. These guns are all worked from the room range finders. The elevation, etc. are all worked from here.

June 19

Had a show and boxing. Was very good. The Capt. on a battleship is like a little king. Everyone stands until he is seated. He has an elevated leather chair above everyone like a throne. Am glad I was not in the navy. Too much of that sort of thing to please me.

June 21

Pernal, one of our boys who had been in the hospital aboard ship got out about 3 AM, but sailors saw him and sent him back. He had nothing on but a life belt. At 4 AM the orderly found his bunk empty. A search of the ship failed to find him. He either jumped or fell overboard as he was never heard of again. We had been losing a lot of souvenirs lately. A search of all our belongings was taken, but nothing came of it. I imagine someone on board ship stole them and hid them on the ship.

June 22

Arose at 3:30 AM. Pulled hammocks to pieces and got our packs fixed up ready for landing. Sighted land as soon as it was light. Thought of the poem, "Breathes there a man with soul so dead," etc. Landed at Newport News at 6 AM Sunday and marched to camp. Our band played all through town and woke people up. Stores close to camp held us up for everything. We were all hungry for pie, and they charged up to $1.50 a pie. Very few of us bought them. A Co. had not spent any of their mess fund overseas, so they had one great big feed at Newport News. How the boys in B Co. did holler. What became of B Co's mess fund? They accused me of getting away with it. They had all forgotten the many big feeds and extra things I had gotten for them in France. That's all the thanks I got for putting myself out to get them better meals. If ever I am in another war, I'll know better. The more you do for a bunch of soldiers, the less they think of you.

June 26

Left Newport News on train with 37th Eng. They had a cooking outfit, so we were free for once. There were about 60 of us. We were all bound for Calif. and the Northwest, arriving at Huntington W.V. just before noon. Stayed about 2 hours. Just before leaving all the boys bound for Missouri came in on another train. Davis, Billyou, and the rest of the cooks were busy in the baggage car getting dinner. It was quite hot and they were sweating profusely, so we gave them the horse laugh. Crossed the Mississippi and on to Cincinnati just before dark. Stayed at Cin. for 4 hours, but were not allowed to leave the train. Passed through Kenova, a town which is in 3 states: Kentucky, Ohio, and Virginia.

June 28

Stayed at Chicago 2 hours. Then on to Omaha where a Sgt. got off and missed the train. He caught us at Ogden, getting on a limited which passed us at Ogden. He went to the Red Cross who gave him $10.00 to pay his fare. He kept the $10.00 and chiseled his way. At Ogden the boys from Portland, Seattle, and points NW left us.

June 30

Arr. At Sacramento 8 PM and Oakland 11 PM. Instead of letting us sleep on the train and cross the bay in the morning, we had to pack up and go across that night. Arr. at the ferry at 11:45, 15 minutes before prohibition went into effect. A big hot meal was awaiting us at the ferry, but the officer in charge would not wait, and we missed it. We went right out to the Presidio in trucks. While at Newport News I had my teeth inspected and the dentist told me to get a bridge and have them all fixed before I was mustered out, so I stayed at the SF Presidio for 3 weeks after the rest of the boys were mustered out. I got my discharge papers July 19, 1919.

While at the Presidio I had all my souvenirs and postcards checked at the YMCA. When I went to get them, they could not be located, so I lost them all. In conclusion, I might say I would not have missed the experience I received in the army for any money. Of course, it worked a hardship on the family, but we all have to suffer more or less at times like these for the good of the country.

G. H. Q.
AMERICAN EXPEDITIONARY FORCES.

GENERAL ORDERS
No. 38-A.

France, February 28, 1919.

MY FELLOW SOLDIERS:

Now that your service with the American Expeditionary Forces is about to terminate, I can not let you go without a personal word. At the call to arms, the patriotic young manhood of America eagerly responded and became the formidable army whose decisive victories testify to its efficiency and its valor. With the support of the nation firmly united to defend the cause of liberty, our army has executed the will of the people with resolute purpose. Our democracy has been tested, and the forces of autocracy have been defeated. To the glory of the citizen-soldier, our troops have faithfully fulfilled their trust, and in a succession of brilliant offensives have overcome the menace to our civilization.

As an individual, your part in the world war has been an important one in the sum total of our achievements. Whether keeping lonely vigil in the trenches, or gallantly storming the enemy's stronghold; whether enduring monotonous drudgery at the rear, or sustaining the fighting line at the front, each has bravely and efficiently played his part. By willing sacrifice of personal rights; by cheerful endurance of hardship and privation; by vigor, strength and indomitable will, made effective by thorough organization and cordial co-operation, you inspired the war-worn Allies with new life and turned the tide of threatened defeat into overwhelming victory.

With a consecrated devotion to duty and a will to conquer, you have loyally served your country. By your exemplary conduct a standard has been established and mantained never before attained by any army. With mind and body as clean and strong as the decisive blows you delivered against the foe, you are soon to return to the pursuits of peace. In leaving the scenes of your victories, may I ask that you carry home your high ideals and continue to live as you have served—an honor to the principles for which you have fought and to the fallen comrades you leave behind.

It is with pride in our success that I extend to you my sincere thanks for your splendid service to the army and to the nation.

Faithfully,

John J. Pershing
Commander in Chief.

OFFICIAL:
ROBERT C. DAVIS,
Adjutant General.

Copy furnished to *Mess Sgt Frank H Watson*
6of th Engineers

Commanding.

The 604th Engineer

VILLIERS-SUR-SUIZE, FRANCE   February 1919   VOLUME I. NUMBER I.

ENGINEERS ARE CORPS FOOTBALL CHAMPS

Six Hundred and Fourth Engineers' Crack Eleven Plows Through for 6-to-0 Victory Over Headquarters Troop, 5th Army Corps.

NOGENT-EN-BASSIGNY, Feb. 1, 1919.—Another victory was added to Dube Ursella's all-star aggregation of football athletes, being the third successive trimming they have handed ambitious aspirants for gridiron honors. Headquarters Troop, 5th Corps, were the victims, 6-0 the score. The 604th Engineers are now corps troop champions of the 5th Corps.

Owing to a sprained knee, Rube did not get into the game, but Hall, who was substituted, proved to be a quarterback of no mean ability. The field was in poor condition, covered with snow, but an enthusiastic crowd was all present and accounted for. This was one occasion when the lowest buck private could slap a colonel on the back, yell "Don't them birds show class?" and get away with it!

And the Band.

What is a football game without a band? Even the loyal supporters of the defeated team found time to gather around the 604th Engineers Regimental Band while said musicians issued beaucoup music.

The Engineers outclassed and outplayed the Headquarters Troop, and plowed their way through the Headquarters defense for a touchdown in the first quarter, Hall carrying the ball.

Schultz Stars for Headquarters Troop.

Much credit must be given to Schultz, the human dynamo in the Headquarters bunch, who proved to be the star of that team, but there were too many engineers in his way. It was some game, and the boys measured up beautifully to the standard set by the 604th Engineers in athletics as well as the pick and shovel.

The lineup:

604th ENGINEERS—(6)		HEADQUARTERS TROOP—(0)
Davis	L. E.	Griffin
Anderson	L. T.	Lester
Dube	L. G.	Clemons
Murphy	C.	Leach
Yarn	R. G.	Schultz
Anderson	R. T.	Lake
Hall	R. E.	Stanforth
Jones	Q. B.	Burley
Lawrence	R. H.	Schultz (captain)
Kameron	L. H.	Lashway
Knott	F. B.	Goldsmith

ANOTHER WAR HORROR.

Mothers, fathers, sweethearts and wives may have their own particular reasons for thankfulness that the war is over, but we of the A. E. F. breathed a special and very big sigh of relief when Bloody Bill shook the dust of Germany from his Number Elevens. For we are slowly being freed of one of the war's most terrible horrors—the magazine cover soldier! For many months have we shivered when he went "over the top," attired in the late lamented campaign hat and canvas leggings—neither of which have ever been seen in the A. E. F. except on the person of some ignorant gink in the S. O. S. And to the gents who have toted "gaspipe" for many a weary mile and shuddered with horror when the C. O. smartly shouted "Rusty bore, no passes," it's rather of a joke to see the magazine heroes shouldering a rifle with Krag-Jorgenson sights, Springfield barrel and Enfield bolt. Shades of Michael Angelo and James Montgomery Flagg—have a heart—you birds of the pen and brush.

OUR NEW CHAPLAIN.

After many months there has come in our midst a brand-new chaplain; about the first thing we ever got that wasn't salvaged and "made over good as new." Chaplain Kemp is a real honest-to-goodness man, a regular fellow, with a cheery

KING OF THE CANTEEN LOSES HIS CROWN

Many Months of Unmolested Reign—His Nibs Dethroned by Forces of the Red Triangle—Feminine Touch Adorns Once Barren Walls.

(Wireless from special Correspondent.)
VILLIERS-SUR-SUIZE, France, Feb. 25, 1919.—Villiers-sur-Suize is all excited and there is a buzzing atmosphere around the canteen that has not been witnessed since it was started. Large forces of men are policing the place, and the ordinary barrenness so much in evidence in the good old days has totally disappeared. There are fancy curtains in the windows, and large posters in gay colors adorn the same walls hitherto decorated with cobwebs.

A Real Woman.

The veteran old Canteen Sergeant Baucom has abdicated in favor of the Y. M. C. A. The new ruler of the canteen is a real, honest-to-goodness American woman—the first that we've seen since we left the Land of Liberty. Miss Olive Williams is her name, and the place that used to require a shovel to force the door is under new rule.

We will no longer have to use our mess kits for writing tables, nor will it be necessary to pull the time-honored alibi to the folks at home for not writing. The place can be swept with a broom now, while we all have memories of the days when nothing short of a Kansas cyclone could extract the cigarette butts, paper wrappers and the like from the corners of the old monarch's throne room.

It must be tough on the veteran old despot to relinquish his crown now, but beauty first, last and always.

Hero Baucom.

We remember the days when it nearly cost a man his life to fall into line for a piece of chocolate, and when the boys eased back in the line 10 or 15 times the old vet faced the barrage like a hero. There were times when we didn't know the meaning of the word chocolate—much less buying it—but we must give Baucom credit for establishing our first overseas canteen, and while he took a great pleasure in rimming us of our hard-earned francs, remember that between the wine shop and him the choice was pretty thin; the francs eventually went to one place or the other.

Baucom wasn't particular what kind of money we gave him—francs, dollars or pounds, it was all the same. Some of the wise ones tried cashing old rent receipts and Chinese laundry tickets, but it wouldn't work. When the men have recovered from the initial shock of having a place to write and read it is generally believed that the regiment will settle down to take things as they come, as of old.

A NEW RECRUIT FOR UNCLE SAM'S ENGINEERS.

On January 29, 1919, in Villiers-sur-Suize, France, the bee got in everybody's bonnet that a regimental paper would fill a long-felt want. As a result "The 604th Engineer" makes its initial bow in this issue. The policy of this paper—for a short time at least—will be that of humor, good fellowship, what news we can gather, and perhaps some constructive criticism of the organization members. Of course, choice bits of scandal will not be overlooked, for the sheet does not depend on advertisers for its subsistence. It is anti-German and pro-Homeseeker.

Until they get too rank the paper will be under the control of a staff headed by Managing Editor, Master Engineer Tom J. Fritz; Editor-in-Chief, Pvt. 1st Cl. B. C. Kiesling, Ordnance Detachment and Headquarters Co.; Assistant Editors, Pvt. Kelley, cartoonist, and Pvt. Fleming, both of Co. A; Sgt. R. H. Daugherty, Co. B; Pvt. Hagan, C Co.

YOU SAID IT, BO!

Members of this outfit are cautioned not to spend money foolishly

Frank, Margaret, and Barney Watson, 1919

AFTERWORD

In May of 2018 I took a *New York Times* Tour of World War I sites in France and Belgium on the 100th anniversary of the end of that war. I was interested in seeing where Grandpa Watson had been and in knowing more about that devastating war.

WWI was the most destructive war in history. It was the first global war, and it shaped the 20th century. Over 10,000,000 people died and 20,000,000 were wounded. In 1918 the Spanish Flu broke out, killing even more people.

Perhaps the worst fighting occurred on the Western Front. By 1918 the troops of England, France, Germany and Italy were exhausted from years of fighting.

America entered the war in April 1917 after hearing that Germany talked with Mexico about Mexico supporting the German side. After the war Germany would help them regain Texas, New Mexico and Arizona.

Americans trained in the South for 6-9 months and then left for overseas. In the beginning, the American troops had no uniforms or artillery. There were not enough ships to transport the men to Europe, so they often relied on British ships.

When the Americans did arrive, they were healthy, fit and ready to fight. Their presence turned the tide on the Western Front. Grandpa was one of those Americans. The troops were racially segregated in the war, but the black soldiers distinguished themselves in battle, and General Pershing strongly supported them.

One of the things that surprised me was the small area of northeastern France and southern Belgium that troops fought over for years. The last 100 days, part of the time Grandpa was there, there were huge losses. 500,000 soldiers lost their lives over a chunk of land outside of Ypres, Belgium that was only 5 miles long and not that wide. There are 197 cemeteries in Ypres.

That is the other thing that astonished me—all the cemeteries. In small villages, there would be several cemeteries, all from veterans of WWI. Near the Argonne Forest there is an American cemetery with 14,000 Americans buried in it.

The Argonne Forest is lovely now with full grown trees, but during the war all the trees were cut down so no one could hide in them. There are steep inclines and valleys throughout. One can imagine how difficult it must have been to fight in the area. There are lots of remains of pits, trenches, fox holes, old barbed wire and shell casings.

The area around Verdun, where Grandpa spent most of his time was beautiful in the spring, rolling green hills, small villages with stone houses that were rebuilt after the war. The countryside is very pastoral, very clean. Looking at it now, it is hard to imagine the destruction of the past.

Some of the tunnels are still in existence. Grandpa mentions the Germans having such nice quarters in these tunnels. Even 100 years later, one could see the differences. The French tunnels were poorly constructed; the English ones were better, but the German ones were the best. They were strongly and neatly built with room for bookcases and other comforts not associated with fighting a war.

We walked through "no man's land," an area 600 meters wide, that separated the Allied troops and the Germans. Drainage systems had been destroyed, so when it rained there was lots of mud. Tanks and other vehicles sometimes couldn't move. Grandpa mentions the rain and the mud.

Grandpa also writes about cooking on rolling wagons. In a museum we saw a couple of those. They were very large wooden carts mounted on iron wagon wheels with a stove and other utensils in them. It is hard to believe one could cook meals for hundreds of men using these.

To this day, one can find stray bullets and other remnants from the war in the fields. Farmers plowing still come across bones of men who fought during that war. The trip was sobering. Seeing the remnants of a horrific war that took place 100 years ago, I thought of President Wilson's words, "a war to end all wars." Except it didn't.

— *Carol Kaplan 2020*

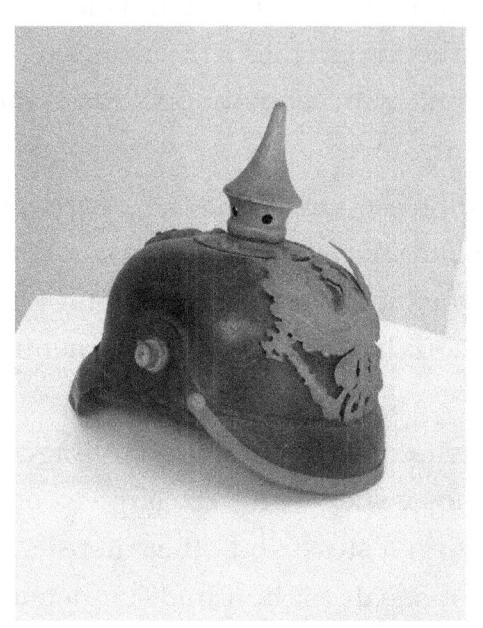

www.ingramcontent.com/pod-product-compliance
Lightning Source LLC
Chambersburg PA
CBHW082104280426
43661CB00089B/849